The Iliad and the Odyssey

adapted from
HOMER

CORE CLASSICS®

ISBN 978-1-68380-615-8
COPYRIGHT © 2020 CORE KNOWLEDGE FOUNDATION
ALL RIGHTS RESERVED
PRINTED IN CANADA

CORE KNOWLEDGE FOUNDATION
801 EAST HIGH STREET
CHARLOTTESVILLE, VIRGINIA 22902

www.coreknowledge.org

TABLE OF CONTENTS

PREFACE BY E.D. HIRSCH, JR.............................I

INTRODUCTION TO GREEK MYTHOLOGY............1
  Two Lasting Epics..1
  The Gods and Goddesses of Greek Mythology..................3
  Godlike Powers and Human Behaviors........................4
  Major Gods and Goddesses......................................5
  Soothsayers and Sacrifices......................................7

A GUIDE TO MAJOR CHARACTERS........................9
  Main Characters in the Iliad....................................9
    Main Greek Characters..9
    Main Trojan Characters......................................10
  Main Characters in the Odyssey..............................11
  Gods, Goddesses, and Other Supernatural Characters......13

Before the Iliad 15
How the Trojan War Began: The Apple of Discord 15
- The Queen's Dream 16
- The Quarrel of the Goddesses 18
- The Judgment of Paris 20
- Helen of Troy 22

The League Against Troy 24
- Reluctant Odysseus 25
- The Hero Achilles 28
- Other Greek Heroes 31

The Trojan War Begins 32
- How They Fought 33

The Invocation of the Muse 36

Selections from the Iliad 39
The Wrath of Achilles 39
The Combat Between Menelaus and Paris 47
How Hector Bade Farewell to Andromache 54
The Battle on the Plain 59
The Ambassadors to Achilles 62
The Wounding of Hector and the Battle at the Ships 68
How Patroclus Went into Battle 74
The Rousing of Achilles 78
The Making of the Arms 82
How Achilles Avenged the Death of Patroclus 87
Priam's Appeal to Achilles 96

AFTER THE ILIAD..102
The Death of Achilles..102
The Wooden Horse...105
The Fall of Troy...109

SELECTIONS FROM THE ODYSSEY......................111
A Visit from a Goddess..111
Telemachus Addresses the Suitors...............................119
Telemachus Prepares for a Voyage..............................126
Telemachus Visits Nestor at Pylos................................130
Telemachus in Sparta...137
A Mother Fears for Her Son...143
Odysseus and Calypso...147
Odysseus and Nausicaa..155
Odysseus and the Phaeacians.......................................163
Odysseus Begins His Story: The Cyclops.....................175
Odysseus Continues His Story: Circe the Enchantress.......186
Odysseus Continues His Story: Of the Sirens and Other Wonders........196
Odysseus Returns to Ithaca..204
Odysseus and the Swineherd.......................................211
Odysseus and Telemachus..215
The Beggar in the House of Odysseus.........................222
Penelope and the Stranger...230
The Trial of the Bow and the Revenge of Odysseus......243
Husband and Wife Together..256
Father and Son..261

PRONUNCIATION GUIDE..268

PREFACE

This book introduces young readers to the *Iliad* and the *Odyssey*, some of the oldest stories we have. Both works were originally very long poems in the Greek language. Here they are presented in shortened versions translated into English and told as stories.

They were first written down more than 2,500 years ago, but the stories were preserved and shared many centuries before that. They tell of events that happened more than 3,000 years ago, in and around the countries we now know as Greece and Turkey. They tell of heroes facing enormous and frightening challenges, and meeting those challenges with bravery, skill, and ingenuity.

If you have learned about Greece in the Classical period or "Golden Age," then you might associate ancient Greece with great works of art such as the Parthenon and with lasting ideas such as democracy. But the *Iliad* and the *Odyssey* tell stories of the Greeks from earlier times—not of artists and philosophers, but of warriors and raiders.

II — THE ILIAD AND THE ODYSSEY

The *Iliad*, a tale of war, describes the feats of individual heroes and the gods on both sides of the conflict. The *Odyssey* tells of one hero's adventures as he and his men try to return home after the war had ended. The forces that opposed them include one-eyed monsters and a sorceress who turns men into pigs.

The glories and trials of war, the adventures of heroes on a mission—people still thrill to such stories. Indeed, hugely popular entertainments such as the *Star Wars* movies have roots in the *Iliad* and the *Odyssey*.

In some ways the *Iliad* and the *Odyssey* may seem as familiar as today's blockbuster movies, but in other ways they are strange and unfamiliar. At one moment the people in these stories may act in ways that we recognize and understand; a moment later, they may do things that startle or shock us. The values they take for granted make us think about what we value as individuals, as members of families and communities, and as human beings.

For example, if a raggedly dressed stranger were to knock at the door of someone's house, how would you expect him to be treated? Today, we might be suspicious or fearful and perhaps turn that person away. But if we lived in Homer's world, an unknown stranger coming to our land could expect help or assistance, which we would readily provide.

Before asking the stranger a single question — even "Who are you?" or "What do you want?" — we would first offer food, drink, and other assistance. We would provide the stranger gifts when he leaves, while the stranger, if able, would offer gifts in return. These rituals of mutual hospitality between host and guest are part of what the ancient Greeks called *xenia* (pronounced **zee-nee-uh**), and it forms an important part of the social world in the *Iliad* and especially in the *Odyssey*.

The world of the *Iliad* and the *Odyssey* is in many ways a male world, in which men ruled and women had limited roles. Even royal women had little power, while women of lower status were generally treated as servants and seen as property. In a wartime raid, the victors might carry off not only treasure but also women as part of the "spoils of war."

Some women in these stories do emerge as

distinct and compelling characters. For example, there is Andromache, wife of the Trojan hero Hector in the *Iliad*, as well as Penelope, wife of the Greek hero Odysseus in the *Odyssey*. Also, the goddess Athena plays an especially active role in the *Odyssey*.

Mostly, though, the *Iliad* and the *Odyssey* show us a male warrior culture that values individual bravery and lasting fame. Achilles, the central figure of the *Iliad*, recalls a prophecy that his mother told him when he was young:

My son, two paths lie before you, and you may choose which you will follow. If you stay in this land and fight against Troy, then you will never go back to your own land but will die in your youth. Only your name will live forever. But if you will leave this land and go back to your home, then you shall live long, even to old age, but your name will be forgotten.

To live long and be forgotten or to die young and be remembered forever — that is the choice Achilles faces. The Greeks called it *kleos* — the lasting glory that gives one a kind of immortality because people will continue to tell your story forever and ever. The heroes of the *Iliad* and the *Odyssey* value the renown that comes from deeds of valor, strength, and ingenuity. And indeed, perhaps they achieved it, for here we are, reading their stories, remembering their names.

Over the years, the fame of the *Iliad* and the *Odyssey* has grown. Both works continue to be read and talked about to this day. They have been translated into many languages and enjoyed by people in many lands. They have inspired modern writers to write new versions of the old adventures, and to imagine the stories from the point of view of characters who are not the central heroes.

The compelling power of the stories keeps us reading them. The *Iliad* and the *Odyssey* show us men and women acting in very human ways, facing and overcoming great challenges, confronting grief and loss, celebrating love and reunions. They are, at once, strange and familiar, distant and close.

E. D. Hirsch Jr.
Spring, 2020

The Iliad and the Odyssey

INTRODUCTION TO GREEK MYTHOLOGY

Two Lasting Epics

An **epic** is a long poem that tells in a grand manner the deeds of great heroes. From ancient times, more than twenty-five hundred years ago, there have come down to us two great epics in the Greek language, the *Iliad* and the *Odyssey*.

The *Iliad* is a tale of war. In this war, known as the Trojan War, a number of Greek kings joined forces and laid **siege** to the city of Troy. The *Iliad* focuses on events that happen in the tenth and final year of the Trojan War. (The title, *Iliad*, comes from the Greek name for Troy, *Ilium*.)

> **siege (seej):** in war, the act of surrounding a place in order to cut it off from outside help and, over time, weaken and capture it

The *Odyssey* tells the story of a journey—the long journey home made by the Greek hero Odysseus after the end of the Trojan War. Along the way, Odysseus has many adventures and suffers dearly before reaching his native land.

(We now use the word *odyssey* to refer to any long, wandering voyage filled with challenges on the way toward reaching a goal.)

Some people think that these two great epics were composed by a blind poet, Homer, in the 8th century **BCE**, who wandered from city to city and earned his living by reciting poems. Most scholars, however, think that that the *Iliad* and the *Odyssey* were not composed by a single poet but represent the work of many poets over a long time, who passed down stories of their heroes by word of mouth from one generation to another. Homer was the person who collected and pulled together the best versions of the various poems.

> **BCE:** Before the Common Era or Before the Current Era

HOMER

Whatever the source of the poems, they must have been told and retold for many years before they were finally written down. This book retells selected adventures from the two epic poems as stories for you to read and enjoy.

The Gods and Goddesses of Greek Mythology

To understand the *Iliad* and the *Odyssey*, you need to know something about the religious beliefs of the ancient Greeks.

If you have studied Greek **myths**, you know that the ancient Greeks believed in many gods and goddesses: a god of war; gods of nature; and gods of music, poetry, dancing, hunting, and other arts and activities. As the ancient Greeks saw it, different gods ruled all parts of the universe: the heavens and the earth, the sun and the moon, the ocean, seas, and rivers, the mountains and forests, the winds and storms.

> **myths:** traditional stories that explain why things happen or how they came to be

The gods also controlled everything that happened to the people living on earth. Indeed, as told in the *Iliad*, nearly everything that happened in the Trojan War was guided by a god or goddess. The epic tells us that the gods helped cause the war and that they took sides, some helping the Greeks and some the Trojans.

Godlike Powers and Human Behaviors

In ancient Greek myths, the gods and goddesses acted in many ways like human beings. They felt strong emotions and often argued among themselves. They married and had children, and needed food and drink and sleep. They drank a delicious wine called nectar, ate a food called ambrosia, and enjoyed never-ending life and youth.

Though the gods could not die, they could be wounded and suffer pain. They often took part in the **quarrels** and wars of people on earth, and they had weapons and armor like human warriors.

quarrels: arguments, disagreements

The ancient Greeks thought their gods and goddesses had great powers. Some could make themselves invisible. Some could change into different forms, for example, into the shape of an animal. When an earthly disaster occurred—a great storm, an earthquake, a shipwreck—people

Introduction to Greek Mythology

thought it was caused by the anger of some god.

The home of most of the gods was on the top of Mount Olympus. Here they lived in golden palaces and feasted together at grand banquets.

In their cities, the ancient Greeks built grand temples for the worship of the gods. One of the most famous was the Parthenon, at Athens. At the **shrines** of the gods people left gifts of gold and silver. On **altars** in the open air, animals were sacrificed to please the gods.

> **shrines:** places thought to be holy, often associated with some specific god or goddess
>
> **altars:** tables used for religious ceremonies

Major Gods and Goddesses

The king of the gods was **Zeus**. He was sometimes called the "Mighty Thunderer." In his anger he hurled lightning bolts down from the heavens.

The wife of Zeus, queen of the gods, was **Hera**. As you shall see, she was the great enemy of Troy and the Trojans. One of the daughters of Zeus, called **Aphrodite**, was the goddess of beauty and love.

Poseidon was the god of the sea. He usually

HERMES, ZEUS, AND ATHENA

carried a three-pointed spear called a trident, a sign of his power over the oceans.

Ares was the god of war and **Hades** the god of the underworld, the regions of the dead. One of the most powerful of the gods was **Apollo**, the god of the sun, and also of medicine, music, and poetry.

Other major gods mentioned in the *Iliad* and the *Odyssey* include **Pallas Athena**, the goddess of wisdom; **Hermes**, the swift-footed messenger god;

and, **Hephaestus**, the god of fire and the **forge** who made thunderbolts for Zeus and weapons of war for earthly heroes.

forge: a furnace for melting metal; also, a blacksmith's workshop

Soothsayers and Sacrifices

The ancient Greeks believed that their gods made their will known to people in various ways; for example, through the behavior of birds, vivid dreams, and sometimes even by appearing in different forms and speaking directly to people.

To understand the will of the gods, the ancient Greeks also turned to **soothsayers**, who had the power of seeing into the future. In temples, priests called oracles gave answers from the gods to people's questions. The best-known oracle of ancient times was in the temple of Apollo at Delphi, in Greece.

soothsayers: persons who were believed to have the power of seeing into the future

The Greeks never engaged in war or any other important undertaking without first sacrificing to the gods. These sacrifices usually took the form of ceremonies in which animals—sheep, goats, pigs, or cattle—were killed, and then parts of the animals burned as offerings to the gods.

If they were defeated in battle, the ancient Greeks saw it as a sign of the anger of Zeus or some other immortal being on Olympus. When making treaties of peace, they called the gods as witnesses and prayed to Zeus to send terrible punishments on any who should break their promises. In the story of the Trojan War you will find many examples of such appeals to the gods by the chiefs on both sides.

A GUIDE TO MAJOR CHARACTERS

Main Characters in the Iliad
Main Greek Characters

ACHILLES (uh-**kil**-eez) The central hero of the *Iliad* and the greatest of the Greek warriors, he is known for his wrath, which, when inflamed by an argument with Agamemnon, brings trouble and sorrow to the Greeks fighting against Troy.

AGAMEMNON (a-guh-**mem**-nahn) The king of Mycenae (my-**see**-nee), elder brother of Menelaus, and commander-in-chief of the Greek forces fighting against Troy, his rash actions provoke a destructive feud with Achilles.

AJAX TELAMON (A-jaks **teh**-luh-mahn) A son of King Telamon, and called "Ajax Telamon" to distinguish him from another warrior also named Ajax, this courageous Greek warrior is a huge man of giant strength.

DIOMEDES (die-uh-**mee**-deez) The young king of Argos, he is known for fighting bravely and speaking his mind in council meetings.

HELEN (**hel**-uhn) The extraordinarily beautiful wife of King Menelaus of Sparta, she is taken to Troy by Paris, thus sparking the Trojan War.

MENELAUS (meh-nuh-**lay**-us) He is the king of Sparta, younger brother of Agamemnon, and husband of Helen.

NESTOR (**nes**-ter) The king of Pylos and a once mighty warrior, he has grown too old to fight but still guides the Greeks with his wise advice.

ODYSSEUS (oh-**dis**-ee-us) The king of Ithaca, known for his bravery and for his clever mind, he is also the central hero of Homer's *Odyssey*.

PATROCLUS (puh-**troh**-klus) The devoted friend and constant companion of Achilles, he is a courageous warrior and commander of the Myrmidons (the army of Achilles).

Main Trojan Characters

ANDROMACHE (an-**drah**-muh-kee) She is the devoted wife of Hector.

CASSANDRA (kuh-**san**-druh) The daughter of King Priam and Queen Hecuba, and the sister of Hector and Paris, she has the gift of prophecy but was cursed by a god so that no one believes her.

CHRYSEIS (kry-**see**-iss) A daughter of Chryses (a priest of Apollo), she is taken captive by Agamemnon.

HECTOR (**hek**-ter) The eldest son of King Hecuba and Queen Priam, he is a prince of Troy and the best and bravest of the Trojan warriors.

Major Characters

HECUBA (**heh**-kyuh-buh) She is the queen of Troy, wife of King Priam, and mother of Hector.

PARIS (**pair**-iss) A prince of Troy and younger brother of Hector, he is known for his beauty more than his bravery.

PRIAM (**pry**-uhm) The king of Troy, husband of Hecuba, and father of many (including Hector and Paris), he is no longer a young man but still a courageous leader.

Main Characters in the Odyssey

ALCINOUS (al-**sin**-oh-us) The king of the seafaring Phaeacians (fee-**aa**-shuns) and father of Nausicaa, he encourages Odysseus to tell his story and helps him return to Ithaca.

ANTINOUS (an-**tin**-oh-us) He is one of the leaders of the suitors who want to marry Penelope.

ARGOS (**ahr**-gos) He is Odysseus' old dog.

EUMAEUS (yoo-**may**-us) He is the old and loyal swineherd who looks after the pigs that belong to Odysseus, and who helps Odysseus overcome the suitors.

EURYCLEIA (yoor-ih-**klee**-uh) A trusted old servant in Odysseus' household, she was nursemaid to both the young Odysseus and his son Telemachus.

EURYMACHUS (yuh-**rim**-uh-kus) He is one of the leaders of the suitors who want to marry Penelope.

LAERTES (lay-**uhr**-teez or lay-**air**-teez) He is the father of Odysseus.

MELANTHIUS (meh-**lan**-thee-us) He is a rude and disloyal goatherd who serves in the household of Odysseus.

MENELAUS (meh-nuh-**lay**-us) He is the king of Sparta who, reunited with his wife Helen after the Trojan War, welcomes Telemachus and tells him what he knows about Odysseus.

NAUSICAA (**nah**-sih-kuh or nah-sih-**kay**-uh) The daughter of King Alcinous and Queen Arete (ahr-**ee**-tee), she helps Odysseus when he comes to Phaeacia.

NESTOR (**nes**-ter) The aged king of Pylos, he has returned home after the Trojan War and welcomes Odysseus's son, Telemachus, who has come to Pylos seeking news of his father.

ODYSSEUS (oh-**dis**-ee-us) The king of the island of Ithaca and central hero of the *Odyssey*, after the Trojan War he uses his wits and courage to return to his wife and homeland, and resume his place as king.

PEISISTRATUS (pie-**sis**-truh-tus) A son of Nestor and prince of Pylos, he becomes a close friend of Telemachus and travels with him in hopes of finding news of Odysseus.

PENELOPE (puh-**nel**-uh-pee) The faithful wife of Odysseus and mother of their son, Telemachus, she uses her wits to put off the suitors pressuring her to choose one of them to marry.

PHILOETIUS (fih-**lee**-shyus) He is the loyal cowherd who looks after the cattle that belong to Odysseus, and who helps Odysseus overcome the suitors.

Major Characters

Telemachus (tuh-**leh**-muh-kus) The son of Odysseus and Penelope, he is at first unsure how to protect his father's kingdom from the suitors, but, guided by the goddess Athena, he grows in wisdom and determination, and eventually helps his father overcome the suitors.

Gods, Goddesses, and Other Supernatural Characters

Aeolus (**ee**-uh-lus) The god of the winds, at first he helps Odysseus, but later refuses to help him.

Aphrodite (af-ruh-**die**-tee) She is the goddess of love and beauty.

Apollo (uh-**pah**-low) He is the powerful god of the sun, and also of medicine, music, poetry, and archery.

Ares (**air**-eez) He is the god of war.

Athena (uh-**thee**-nuh) A favorite daughter of Zeus, she is the goddess of wisdom who helps both Odysseus and his son Telemachus.

Calypso (kuh-**lip**-so) She is the goddess who holds Odysseus captive for seven years.

Circe (**sur**-see) She is the goddess and enchantress who turns some of Odysseus' men into swine.

Hades (**hay**-deez) He is the ruler of the underworld and god of the dead.

HEPHAESTUS (hih-**feh**-stus) The god of fire and the forge, he makes thunderbolts for Zeus and sometimes weapons of war for earthly heroes.

HERA (**hair**-ah) She is queen of the gods and the wife of Zeus.

HERMES (**her**-meez) He is a messenger of the gods, and also the god of wealth, luck, and thieves.

IRIS (**eye**-ris) She is a messenger of the gods.

POLYPHEMUS (pah-luh-**fee**-mus) He is a one-eyed flesh-eating giant, also known as the Cyclops, who traps Odysseus and some of his men in a cave.

POSEIDON (puh-**sigh**-dun) The brother of Zeus and god of the sea and earthquakes, he is angry with Odysseus and seeks to prevent him from returning to his homeland of Ithaca.

THETIS (**thee**-tis) She is a goddess of the sea and the mother of Achilles.

ZEUS (zoose) He is the mighty king of the gods, husband of Hera, and father of Athena, Aphrodite, Ares, and Apollo.

BEFORE THE *ILIAD*

How the Trojan War Began: The Apple of Discord

In ancient times, the great city of Troy was located on the northwest coast of the land now known as Turkey. The city stood at the foot of Mount Ida, near the shores of the Aegean Sea. Strong walls protected the city from its enemies.

In the years before the Trojan War began, the city enjoyed peace and prosperity under the rule of King Priam and his wife, Queen Hecuba. They had many children, among them a beautiful daughter named Cassandra.

The god Apollo loved Cassandra so much that he offered to grant her any wish. Cassandra asked for the power of prophecy, the ability to see into the future.

Apollo gave her this gift, but then she angered the god. Apollo could not take back his gift, but he proclaimed that no one should ever believe Cassandra or pay any attention to her predictions, even though they were true. And so when Cassandra predicted the evils that were to come upon Troy, even her own people did not believe her.

The eldest son of King Priam and Queen Hecuba was Hector, the noblest of the Trojan heroes. A younger son, Paris, would bring sorrow and disaster to Troy.

The Queen's Dream

Just before Paris was born, a strange thing troubled the family of old King Priam. Queen Hecuba had a dream in which she saw her newborn babe turn into a flaming torch that burned up the walls and the high towers of Troy. She told the king her dream. When the child was born, they called a soothsayer and asked him what the dream meant.

"It means," he said, "that if this babe lives, he shall be a torch to turn the walls and high towers of Troy into heaps of ashes."

"But what can be done to prevent this terrible thing?" asked Priam.

"The child must not live," answered the soothsayer.

In great sorrow, Priam called his master shepherd and told him to take the child into the thick woods, leaving him alone on the slopes of Mount Ida, where he would not live long without care and nourishment.

The shepherd did as he was commanded. He laid the infant by a tree and then hurried away. But the spirits who haunt the woods and groves saw the babe. They pitied and cared for the babe. Some brought it honey from the bees, some fed it with milk from the goats, and some protected it from the wolves and bears.

After five days, the shepherd, who could not stop thinking about the babe, came back to the place where he had left him. Fearing the worst, he glanced toward the foot of the tree. To his surprise, the babe was still there. It looked up and stretched its plump hands toward him.

The shepherd's heart would not let him turn away. He took the child in his arms and carried it to his own humble home in the valley, and there he brought it up as his own son. The boy grew to be tall and brave, and a great help to the shepherds around Mount Ida.

One day, as young Paris tended his sheep, he met Oenone, a river **nymph** of Mount Ida. Day after day he sat with her near her woodland home.

Soon, Paris and Oenone were wedded. Neither of them dreamed that any sorrow would come their way. But sorrow would come, and its cause lay in a quarrel among three goddesses, Hera, Aphrodite, and Athena.

> **nymph:** in mythology, a nature spirit in the form of a beautiful young girl

The Quarrel of the Goddesses

The quarrel among the three goddesses began during the marriage between Peleus and Thetis. Peleus was the king of the land called Thessaly in Greece. Thetis was a beautiful sea nymph, one of the immortals. Although Thetis did not want to marry a mortal man, she at last consented. Kings and queens from near and far came to their wedding feast, and all the gods were invited—all except one.

The one exception was Eris, the goddess of **discord**. Eris had once lived on Olympus, but she caused so much trouble that Zeus **banished** her forever.

> **discord:** disagreement, conflict
>
> **banished:** sent away as a punishment

Angry that she had not been invited to the wedding, Eris decided to disturb the marriage feast. She suddenly appeared and threw on a table a beautiful golden apple, on which were **inscribed** these words: *For the fairest*.

> **inscribed:** written, engraved

Just as Eris planned, the wedding feast broke into loud arguments. Athena, goddess of wisdom, claimed the prize, but Hera, wife of Zeus and queen of the gods, refused to listen. Aphrodite, goddess of beauty, said that the apple obviously belonged to her.

Discord had indeed come to the wedding feast. Who should have the apple "for the fairest"? Not one of the gods dared to decide so dangerous a question—not even Zeus himself.

Zeus knew that whatever he might decide, he would be sure to offend two of the three goddesses. And so the task of judging which goddess was the fairest was given to a mortal, the handsome young shepherd of Mount Ida, Paris.

The Judgment of Paris

One warm afternoon, Paris sat in the shade of a tree at the foot of Mount Ida. As his flocks grazed upon the hillside, he heard what sounded like sweet music. He raised his eyes and gasped to see three immortals standing before him — Hera, Athena, and Aphrodite.

They told him of their argument and handed him the golden apple. And they asked him to give the apple to the one whom he judged to be the fairest.

Hera said, "Paris, give me the prize and you will have wealth and kingly power."

Then gray-eyed Athena spoke: "Be wise and honor me, Paris," she said. "I will give you wisdom that shall last forever, and great glory among men."

Last of all spoke Aphrodite, whose beauty dazzled the young shepherd into wide-eyed amazement: "Give me the prize," she said, "and you shall have for your wife the most beautiful woman in the world."

At these words, the shepherd fell on his knees and placed the golden apple in Aphrodite's hands.

He hardly noticed as the two other goddesses vanished in a dark cloud.

And so, determined to seek his **destiny**, Paris made his way to the city of Troy. At that time, King Priam of Troy was holding a great feast at which the princes and other young men of the land were competing in games of athletic skill. At these games, everybody admired the noble appearance of Paris, though nobody knew who he was. In the competitions he won all the first prizes, for Aphrodite had given him godlike strength and swiftness. He defeated even Hector, who was the greatest athlete of Troy.

> **destiny:** what will happen to a person in the future, as determined by some higher power or unseen plan

"Who are you?" asked the king of the handsome **victor**.

> **victor:** winner

"Before this day," answered Paris, "I tended the flocks and herds on Mount Ida."

Hector, who was **furious** because he had not won a prize, came forward to argue with Paris. Suddenly old Priam cried, "Hector, stand close to the young shepherd, and let us look at you." Turning to his wife, Hecuba, Priam asked, "Did you ever see two so

> **furious:** extremely angry

nearly alike? The shepherd is not as tall, but they have the same eyes, the same smile, the same walk. Ah, what if our young babe did not die after all?"

Then Priam's daughter Cassandra, who had the gift of prophecy, cried out, "Oh, this young shepherd is the child you sent to sleep the sleep of death on Ida's wooded slopes!"

King Priam and Queen Hecuba joyfully welcomed their son. Everybody rejoiced except Cassandra. She knew the evil that Paris would bring to Troy, and she tried to warn them, but nobody would believe what she said.

And so Paris was taken into his father's house and given a place of honor. And he forgot his fair young wife Oenone, leaving her to loneliness among the woods and streams of Mount Ida.

Helen of Troy

Paris took his place as a prince of the royal house of Troy. Always in his mind was the promise made to him on Mount Ida—that he would have the most beautiful woman in the world for his wife. Under the guidance of Aphrodite, Paris set sail for the part of ancient Greece called Sparta, for there lived a woman celebrated for her matchless beauty. This was Helen, wife of Menelaus, king of Sparta.

Landing in Sparta, Paris hurried to the court of King Menelaus. The king gave banquets in his honor. Helen, the beautiful queen, joined in her husband's kind attentions to their guest.

Soon after the arrival of Paris, King Menelaus was called away to the island of Crete. Taking advantage of the absence of Menelaus, Paris persuaded Helen to leave her husband and go with him to Troy. He told her of the promise Aphrodite had made to him, assuring Helen that she would be received with great honor and protected against the anger of Menelaus.

And so Paris took Helen back to Troy with him. At the same time he stole gold treasures and other costly things that belonged to King Menelaus.

After a stormy voyage by sea, Paris and Helen at last reached Troy. They were welcomed with rejoicing by King Priam and Queen Hecuba. In a short time they were married.

Hector, eldest son of Priam, was angry with

Paris for what he had done. He advised King Priam to send Helen back to Sparta. But Priam would not listen, and so Helen remained in Troy.

Priam should have listened, for the act of carrying off Helen would soon spark war between the Trojans and the Greeks.

The League Against Troy

When he heard what Paris had done, Menelaus immediately returned to Sparta. He called upon the other kings and princes of Greece to join him in a war against Troy. He reminded them of the promise they had made when Helen had married Menelaus.

What was that promise and how did it come about? Before she married Menelaus, Helen had been **wooed** by many of the greatest heroes of Greece. Her father wanted to keep peace among all those whom Helen did not choose to marry. So he had all Helen's **suitors** pledge that they would respect her choice of a husband. Moreover, they promised that

> **wooed:** past tense of *woo*—to *woo* is to try to win someone's affection, with the intention of marriage
>
> **suitors:** men who try to win a woman's hand in marriage

if Helen were ever stolen away from her husband, they would help to right such a wrong.

Now that Paris had taken Helen, Menelaus asked the kings and princes of Greece to honor their promise. These men decided that before declaring war against Troy they would seek a peaceful solution. They sent **ambassadors** to Troy to demand that Paris return Helen and the treasures that he had stolen.

ambassadors: persons sent to represent another person, or to represent one country to another

When the Greek ambassadors arrived in Troy, they were welcomed with respect. But King Priam, blinded by his love for Paris, refused the demands of the ambassadors. And so the ambassadors returned home, and at once the kings and princes of Greece began to prepare for war.

Reluctant Odysseus

Years passed as the Greeks prepared a vast force of more than a thousand ships to carry their warriors across the Aegean Sea to the Trojan shores. Some of the Greek kings were **reluctant** to join the

reluctant: unwilling, hesitant

expedition, as they knew that the struggle would be long and **perilous**.

> **expedition:** a journey with a mission or purpose
> **perilous:** dangerous

> **"The face that launched a thousand ships"**
> Around the year 1600, an English playwright wrote a play in which a character refers to Helen of Troy by asking, "Was this the face that launched a thousand ships?" Today, people still sometimes describe a person of great beauty as having a "face that launched a thousand ships."

One such reluctant Greek leader was Odysseus, king of Ithaca. He would gladly have remained in his happy island home with his young wife, Penelope, and his infant son, Telemachus, both of whom he loved dearly.

Odysseus was famed not only for **valor** in war but also for his active mind, always ready with a clever plan to meet any challenge. When the call went out for the Greek leaders to

> **valor:** courage, especially in battle

assemble their fleets at the port of Aulis on the east coast of Greece, although Odysseus paid no attention, the other Greek kings were not willing to continue without so brave and clever a man as Odysseus.

Menelaus himself went to Ithaca to persuade Odysseus to join the expedition against Troy. Along with Menelaus went his brother, Agamemnon, king of Mycenae and one of the most powerful and wealthy of the Greek rulers.

When Odysseus heard of their arrival in Ithaca, he came up with a **scheme** to trick them by pretending to be insane. He dressed in his best clothes and **yoked** an ox and a mule to a plow. Then he went down to the seashore and began to plow the beach, scattering salt upon the sand instead of seed.

> **scheme:** a clever and usually secret plan
>
> **yoked:** connected an animal to a plow by means of a wooden frame placed around the neck

Menelaus and Agamemnon were alarmed at the sight of Odysseus plowing the sand. But one of the followers of Menelaus, a warrior named Palamedes, thought Odysseus might be playing a trick upon them. Palamedes took Odysseus's infant son, Telemachus, from the arms of his **nurse** and placed the babe on the sand in the path of the ox and mule pulling the plow. Odysseus quickly turned the animals aside to avoid injuring his child, thus proving that he was not mad but in full possession of his senses.

> **nurse:** here refers to a person who cares for young children

And so Odysseus had no choice but to join the expedition to Troy. With twelve well-manned

ODYSSEUS, PRETENDING TO BE MAD, SWERVES THE PLOW AWAY FROM HIS SON, THUS PROVING HE IS NOT MAD.

ships he sailed from his rugged island, which he did not see again for twenty years. Ten years he spent at the siege of Troy, and ten on his homeward voyage, during which he met with the adventures described in the *Odyssey*.

The Hero Achilles

Besides Odysseus, another Greek hero was tricked into joining the forces against Troy. This

Before the Iliad

was Achilles, the most renowned warrior of the Trojan War and the principal hero of Homer's *Iliad*.

Achilles was born the son of Peleus and Thetis—their marriage feast, you remember, had been **disrupted** by Eris and the apple of discord.

> **disrupted:** broken apart, thrown into disorder

When Achilles was an infant, Thetis dipped him in the waters of the Styx, the river that (so the Greeks believed) formed the border between the underworld and the world of the living. Any mortal dipped in these waters would be safe from harm from any weapon.

But when Thetis plunged her baby into the dark waters of the Styx, she held him by the foot, and the magical water did not touch the child's heel. And so, many years later, in this one **vulnerable** spot on his body, Achilles would receive the wound from which he died.

> **vulnerable:** capable of being harmed or wounded

Although she had tried to protect her son by dipping him in the Styx, Thetis was afraid to let

> **Achilles' Heel**
> We now use the expression "Achilles' heel" to refer to a person's particular weakness or vulnerability.

Achilles go to the Trojan War, for Zeus had told her that if Achilles took part in the war, he would be killed. When Thetis heard that the Greeks were gathering their forces to attack Troy, she secretly sent her son to the island of Scyros across the sea. She hid him among the daughters of the king of that island. To make sure no one recognized him, she had Achilles dress like a young girl.

A soothsayer told the Greek leaders that without the help of Achilles, Troy could not be taken. Odysseus took on the task of finding Achilles. After much **inquiry** he discovered that Achilles was at Scyros, disguised among the king's daughters. He made his way to the island, where he faced a new difficulty. He had never before seen the young prince, so how was he to know him?

inquiry: seeking information, questioning

As always, the ready mind of Odysseus came up with a plan. He dressed himself as a **peddler** and went to the royal palace, where he displayed fine jewelry to attract the attention of the ladies of the family.

peddler: a traveling seller of goods

The **maidens** gathered about him and began examining the jewels. But one

maidens: young women (especially unmarried ones)

of the group, a tall maiden, stood aside and showed little interest. Then Odysseus drew from his pack a gleaming sword. The tall maiden eagerly seized the weapon, and handled it with much skill and pleasure. The pretend peddler revealed himself as Odysseus and told Achilles why he had come.

Achilles gladly agreed to join his countrymen in their war against Troy. His mother, Thetis, told him of Zeus's prophecy and pleaded with him not to go. But Achilles longed for battle. He soon sailed for Aulis with the brave Myrmidons, as his soldiers were called, accompanied also by his devoted friend and constant companion, Patroclus.

Other Greek Heroes

Agamemnon, who had been chosen as the commander in chief of the Greek forces, sailed with a hundred ships from his kingdom of Mycenae. His brother Menelaus, eager for **vengeance** upon the Trojans, sailed with sixty ships and a strong force of brave Spartans.

Among the other warriors who joined the

> **vengeance:** revenge; getting back at someone; punishing someone for an injury done to you

expedition against Troy was Nestor, known for his **eloquence** and wisdom. And, next to Achilles, the bravest of all the Greeks was Ajax Telamon, a huge man of giant strength.

> **eloquence:** the ability to speak well and persuasively

When all the Greek kings and princes were assembled at Aulis, the **fleet** numbered more than 1,100 ships, according to the account given in the *Iliad*. The total number of men that the ships carried was probably not less than 100,000. Such was the mighty force that the ancient Greeks assembled to punish Troy for the crime committed by Paris.

> **fleet:** a group of ships sailing together

> **As Old as Nestor**
> The ancients believed that Nestor outlived three generations of men, or almost three hundred years. From this it was a custom of the ancient Greeks and Romans, when wishing a long and happy life to their friends, to wish them to live as long as Nestor.

The Trojan War Begins

The Greek chiefs set sail with their large fleet. After a difficult voyage with many setbacks, the fleet reached the coast of Troy.

The Greek warriors poured from their ships and encountered the Trojans in fierce battle. The Trojans were well prepared, for King Priam had called on the princes and chiefs of Troy and neighboring lands, and they had brought large armies to stand against the Greeks. The greatest of the heroes who defended Troy was Priam's son, brave Hector.

In this first battle the Greeks were victorious. After the defeat, the Trojans were unable to keep up the fight in the open **plain** against the vast numbers of the Greeks. They drew their forces inside the strong-walled city.

> **plain:** a large flat area of land

And so began the long siege of Troy. The Greeks hauled their ships out of the water and set large wooden beams to support them upright on the beach. On the plain between this line of Greek ships and the walls of Troy—a distance of a few miles—many a fierce conflict took place, and many a brave warrior fell.

How They Fought

For more than nine years the siege wore on without one side or the other gaining any **decisive** victory. The Trojans were protected by their walls, which the Greeks were unable to break down.

> **decisive:** producing a definite result

In the Trojan War, success depended on the skill and **strategy** of the chiefs, and on the bravery of the soldiers in face-to-face combat. The Greek and Trojan warriors fought with swords, axes, bows and arrows, and long, sharp-pointed spears. Sometimes they used their powerful arms to hurl huge stones. They had shields of circular or oval shape, which they wore on the arm, and which they could move to protect almost any part of the body.

> **strategy:** plan of action; overall planning of military operations

They wore armor. Their chests were covered by metal plates called breastplates. Metal plates called greaves protected their legs from the knees to the feet. On their heads they wore helmets, usually made of metal and decorated on top with a line of animal hair, fur, or feathers.

While most soldiers fought on foot, the chiefs fought in **chariots**, from which they hurled their spears at the enemy. The chariots, pulled by two or three horses, carried two warriors, both standing. The charioteer, or driver, was generally the companion or friend

> **chariots:** two-wheeled horse-drawn vehicles, open at the back, used in ancient warfare and sporting events

of the warrior who stood behind him. Sometimes the warriors came down from their chariots and fought hand to hand with the enemy.

FROM HORSE-DRAWN CHARIOTS, WARRIORS HURLED SPEARS AT THEIR ENEMIES.

During the long siege of Troy, the Greeks sometimes sent part of their forces to raid neighboring lands that were **allies** of Troy. When the Greeks raided a town, they carried off treasures as well as food, wine, and other supplies. Following the practice of the time, they also captured many people, either to sell into slavery or keep in their own service. Once they returned

allies: countries or other groups joining together usually for military support

to their camp, they divided the **spoils** among the chiefs, with the first choice going to the leader of the Greek forces, Agamemnon.

> **spoils:** goods and valuables taken from an enemy in war

In the tenth year of the Trojan War, during one of these raids, two young women were captured. A great quarrel over these two women arose between King Agamemnon, commander of all the Greek forces, and Achilles.

This is the point—with the siege of Troy in its tenth year— at which the *Iliad* begins.

The Invocation of the Muse

Imagine a crowd gathering long, long ago in a city on the shores of the shining Aegean Sea. The audience eagerly waits to hear a blind poet named Homer tell beloved stories of the great deeds of their heroic ancestors in the Trojan War.

Homer begins by asking a goddess—one of the nine **Muses**—to help him tell his story. In Greek mythology, the Muses were daughters of Zeus who inspired poets, singers, and other artists. There was a muse of dance, a muse of history, and muses for different kinds of poetry.

Since Homer's time, poets writing epics have begun their poems with an **invocation of the muse**. An invocation is the act of asking for help or support, often as a prayer to some divine power.

Imagine you are part of that crowd long ago. A hush falls as Homer asks the muse to sing through him, the poet, the story of the wrath—the great anger—of Achilles, and what resulted from it.

And so the story begins...

The Greeks outside Troy

SELECTIONS FROM THE *ILIAD*

*Sing, O goddess, of the wrath of Achilles, son of Peleus, which brought countless **woes** upon the Greeks, and hurled many valiant heroes down to Hades, leaving their bodies as prey to dogs and birds—for such was the will of Zeus, ever since the quarrel began between Achilles and Agamemnon.*

woes: heavy troubles; great sadness

The Wrath of Achilles

For more than nine years the Greeks surrounded and attacked the city of Troy, but they could not break through the strong walls. They had been away from their homes for so long that they often needed food, clothes, and other supplies. They left one part of the army to watch the city, and with the other part went about and raided towns and cities.

Because of two maidens taken captive by the Greeks in these raids, a great quarrel began between Achilles and Agamemnon. One of the maidens was called Chryseis and the other Briseis.

Briseis had been given to Achilles, and Chryseis to Agamemnon.

The father of Chryseis was the priest Chryses, who was devoted to the god Apollo. Chryses was deeply saddened by the capture of his daughter. He brought gold and valuable gifts to King Agamemnon and, at a gathering of the Greek chiefs, he begged them to release her.

Many of the chiefs were moved to pity and willing to grant his request. But Agamemnon angrily refused.

"Go away, old man!" cried Agamemnon, "and don't come back, or it will be the worse for you, even though you are a priest. As for your daughter, I will carry her back with me when I have taken Troy."

Chryses left the Grecian camp. As he returned home in sorrow, he prayed to Apollo to punish the Greeks.

Apollo heard his prayer. The god was very angry that his priest should suffer such insults. And so Apollo sent a deadly **plague** upon the Grecian army.

plague: a disease that spreads quickly and often kills those who catch it

With his silver bow, Apollo darted his terrible arrows among the Greeks. For nine days the arrows of death rained down upon the Greek army. On the tenth day of the plague, Achilles called an **assembly**. When the Greek chiefs had gathered, Achilles spoke to them.

assembly: a gathering to discuss problems and make decisions

"Many are **slain** by the arrows of death," said Achilles. "Let us ask the **soothsayers** why Apollo is angry with us."

slain: killed

soothsayers: persons who were believed to have the power of seeing into the future

Then the soothsayer Calchas stood up and said, "Achilles, I can say why the god is angry with us. But I fear I will anger King Agamemnon. Promise me your protection and I will say why this plague has come upon the Greeks."

"Fear nothing, Calchas," answered Achilles. "While I am alive, no one shall harm you, not even Agamemnon himself."

Calchas spoke: "Apollo is angry because his priest has been dishonored by Agamemnon. There is only one way to **appease** the angry god. You must send the girl Chryseis back to her father, with many gifts to be offered to Apollo."

appease: to make someone less angry, to calm someone

Agamemnon leaped up. "Prophet of evil!" he shouted at the soothsayer. "Never have you spoken anything good for me. And now you say I must give up the maiden. Since I do not want to see our people **perish**, I will do so. But I must have another prize."

perish: die, be killed

Achilles responded, "You are too greedy, King Agamemnon. How can we give you a prize since all the spoils have already been divided? Be satisfied and let the maiden go. When we have taken the strong city of Troy, we will make it up to you many times over."

"For now," said Agamemnon, "let the girl be sent back to her father, so that the anger of Apollo may be appeased. After that, if the Greeks give me a suitable prize, I will be content. But if not, I will take it from you, Achilles."

Enraged, Achilles cried out, "Never was there a king so greedy of gain! The Trojans have done no wrong to me. I have been fighting them for your sake and your brother's, while you sit in your tent at ease. But when the spoils are divided, you get the **lion's share**. And now you say you will take the

enraged: filled with violent anger

lion's share: the largest part

little that was given to me. I will not stay here to be shamed and robbed."

"Go, then," said Agamemnon, "and take your ships and soldiers with you. I have other chiefs here who will honor me. But I will take the girl Briseis, who was given to you. If I have to, I will come and fetch her myself. For you must learn that I am in charge here."

In fury, Achilles reached for his sword and said to himself, "Now I will **slay** this villain where he stands." But at that moment the goddess Athena appeared behind him and caught him by his long yellow hair. She had been sent by Hera, queen of the gods, to calm Achilles. (Ever since the day on which Paris made his choice on Mount Ida, when he gave the apple "for the fairest" to Aphrodite, both Athena and Hera hated Troy, the city to which Paris belonged. And so they wished to avoid any **strife** among the Greek chiefs, which would prevent them from defeating Troy.)

slay: kill

strife: conflict, angry disagreement

Achilles was astonished to see the goddess Athena, who appeared to him alone and was invisible to all the rest. He instantly knew who she

Athena stops Achilles, about to draw his sword against Agamemnon.

was and said to her, "O goddess, have you come to see this villain die?"

"No," said Athena. "I have come to calm your anger. You are dear to me, and to Queen Hera. Put away your sword. Say what you feel, but **refrain** from violence."

refrain: to stop yourself from doing something

Achilles put his sword back into its **sheath**, and the goddess swiftly returned to Olympus. Then Achilles addressed Agamemnon in bitter words: "Drunkard with the eyes of a dog and the heart of a deer, hear what I tell you now! One day, and soon, the Greeks will miss Achilles. When you see your people falling by the swords of the Trojans, you will be sorry that you have done this wrong to the bravest man in your army."

> **sheath:** a case for the blade of a sword or knife

Then wise old Nestor rose to speak. He urged the two chiefs to stop quarreling with each other. "King Agamemnon," said Nestor, "do not take from Achilles the prize that the Greeks gave him. And you, Achilles, pay due respect to him who is here the king over all other kings of Greece."

Then Agamemnon said, "The gods have made Achilles a great warrior, but he must learn that there is one here better than he."

"You better than me!" cried Achilles. "What the Greek chiefs gave me, let them take away if

> **Many City-States:** In ancient times, Greece was not a unified nation with a single leader but a group of independent city-states. Achilles and Agamemnon were equals in that they were both kings. But Agamemnon had been appointed the commander of the Greek forces that had joined together to fight against Troy.

they will. But if you, Agamemnon, lay your hands on anything that is my own, in that hour you will die."

And so the assembly was broken up, with Agamemnon and Achilles still **at odds**. Immediately afterwards, the maiden Chryseis was taken back to her father. The anger of the god Apollo was appeased, and the plague ended.

> **at odds:** in a state of conflict or disagreement

Then Agamemnon proceeded to carry out his threat against Achilles. He called two of his officers and said to them, "Go to the tent of Achilles, and fetch the fair Briseis. And if he will not let her go, say that I will come with others to take her."

So the officers went, but much against their will. They found Achilles sitting between his tent and his ship. And they stood in great fear and shame. But when he saw them he spoke kind words to them, though his heart was full of rage.

"Come near," he said. "It is not your fault that you were sent on this errand."

Then Achilles turned to his dear friend, Patroclus, and said, "Bring Briseis from her tent. And let these men be witnesses of how this tyrant king has insulted me, so that they may remember it when he needs my help but shall not have it."

So Patroclus brought Briseis to the officers. And she went with them, much against her will, and often looking back.

Thus began the quarrel that brought countless woes upon the Greeks, for Achilles **vowed** that he would no longer lead his Myrmidons to battle for a king who had so dishonored him.

vowed: made a serious promise

The Combat Between Menelaus and Paris

Agamemnon met with the Greek chiefs, who soon called their armies to battle. Many brave warriors were there, but none that could compare with Achilles, who sat apart and refused to fight.

The leaders of Troy were also gathering their forces within the city. From their walls they had observed the movements of the Greeks, and Zeus had sent a messenger to tell them to get ready for battle.

On the plain before the city walls, the two great armies advanced. As the armies approached each other, Paris rushed forward from the Trojan lines and challenged the Greeks to send their bravest warrior to fight him in **single combat**. His challenge was speedily answered by Menelaus. Menelaus leapt from his chariot, eager for **revenge** on the man who had so greatly wronged him.

> **single combat:** a fight between two people, one against the other
>
> **revenge:** getting back at someone; punishing someone for an injury done to you

When Paris saw Menelaus, a great fear seized him and he ran back to his companions. The noble Hector spoke to his brother in angry words.

"Paris," said Hector, "you are good to look at, but you are worth nothing. You have brought evil on your father, your city, and your people, by carrying away a beautiful woman from her husband, yet you now fear to meet him in battle. It would have been better if you had never been born than to bring such disgrace upon us all."

Paris answered, "You speak the truth, great Hector. But now, listen to me. Let Menelaus meet me in single combat—we will fight man to man. If he kills me, let him take Helen and all her possessions and leave. But if I kill him, then she shall stay here. So, whatever may happen, either way you will live in peace."

Hector, pleased by what Paris had said, went along the line of the Trojans, holding his spear in the middle. He did this to show that he was not meaning to fight, and to keep his men in their places so that they should not begin the battle.

Seeing Hector approach, Agamemnon cried out, "Hold! Great Hector has something to say."

"Hear me, Trojans and Greeks," cried Hector. "Paris, who is the cause of this quarrel between us, says this: 'Let Menelaus meet me in single combat. Everyone else, whether Greek or Trojan, shall lay his arms upon the ground, and look on while we two fight together. For the fair Helen and her riches we two will fight, and the rest will cease from war.'"

When Hector had spoken, King Menelaus stood up and said, "The Greeks and Trojans should be at peace, for there is no quarrel between them. This is my affair. Let me fight Paris alone, and let him be slain whose destiny it is to die. And now let us make a sacrifice to the gods, and swear a great **oath** that we will keep our agreement. Only let King Priam

oath: a promi__ usually cal_ upon some power as a _

himself come and take the oath, for he is to be trusted."

So spoke Menelaus, and both the armies were glad, for they were tired of the war.

Hector sent messengers to King Priam. At this time, Priam was looking out from the high walls of Troy. With him were other princes of the city, old men who could no longer fight. And walking toward them was Helen, who had come to the wall to see the army of the Greeks.

When one of the old princes saw the fair Helen approach, he said to another, "See how beautiful she is! And yet it would be better that she should go back to her own country, rather than staying here and bringing a curse upon us and our children."

The messengers sent by Hector arrived and told King Priam that he was wanted on the plain below to approve the terms of the challenge. Immediately the king mounted his chariot and drove to where Agamemnon waited. A bowl was brought forth, and in it wine from each side, Greek and Trojan, was mixed together. Then Agamemnon, stretching forth his hands, prayed aloud.

"O mighty Zeus!" said Agamemnon. "We call upon you, and upon the Sun, who beholds all things, to be witnesses to this agreement. If Paris slay Menelaus, let him keep Helen and all her possessions, and let us return home in our ships. But if Menelaus slay Paris, let the Trojans give back Helen and all her treasures."

Then the kings drank of the mixed wine, while the Greeks and Trojans joined in praying that terrible punishment might be sent upon any person who might break the agreement.

When this was done, King Priam said, "I will go back to Troy, for I could not bear to see my dear son fighting with Menelaus." So he climbed into the chariot and with troubled thoughts returned to the high-walled city.

Then Hector put two pebbles into a helmet, one for Paris and one for Menelaus. These he shook, looking away as he did, for it was agreed that the man whose pebble first flew out of the helmet would be the first to **cast** his spear at the other.

cast: throw

The pebble of Paris flew out first. The two warriors armed themselves and stood facing each other. First Paris threw his spear. It hit the shield of Menelaus but did not pierce it.

Then Menelaus hurled his spear. It went right through the shield of Paris, and through the armor that he wore upon his body. But Paris bent himself sideways and so escaped the full force of the weapon.

Then Menelaus drew his sword and struck the helmet of Paris with a great blow, but the sword broke into pieces. Menelaus rushed upon Paris and caught him by the horsehair **crest** of his helmet, and dragged him towards the army of the Greeks.

> **crest:** a decorative line of animal hair, fur, or feathers on top of a helmet

Paris struggled as the strap of the helmet choked him. He would have been taken prisoner and killed had not the goddess Aphrodite come to his aid. She broke the strap under his chin, and the helmet came off in the hand of Menelaus.

Grabbing another spear, Menelaus rushed furiously at Paris. But the goddess covered Paris with a mist, snatched him away, and set him down in his own house at Troy.

Menelaus looked all around but he could not

find Paris. Furious as a lion, he paced up and down the field, but not even the Trojans knew where Paris was.

With Paris nowhere to be found, the Greeks claimed the victory for Menelaus. Agamemnon cried out, "Now you Trojans must keep your promise. You must give back fair Helen and her treasures, and we will take her and leave you in peace."

But such was not the will of the gods. **Fate** had **decreed** the destruction of Troy, and so the war could not have a peaceful ending.

> **fate:** the unseen power believed by some to control events and determine what will happen
>
> **decreed:** ordered

From the halls of Olympus, Athena came down and took the form of a youth, a son of King Priam. In this shape she approached Pandarus, a great archer, who could shoot an arrow with as good an aim as any among the Trojan allies. She urged him to aim an arrow at Menelaus.

"You will have gifts from all the Trojans," said Athena, "if you slay Menelaus, and from Paris you may expect splendid gifts indeed."

But Athena, who favored the Greeks, did not really wish that Menelaus should be killed.

And so when Pandarus shot his arrow, she flew to Menelaus and kept the arrow from doing him deadly harm. She guided it to a space between the belt and the breastplate of his armor. There it struck and, piercing the skin, made the red blood gush out.

When Agamemnon, who was standing near, saw the blood, he cried, "Oh, my brother, it was foolish of me to make a **pact** with the Trojans, for they are wicked men and break their oaths!"

pact: agreement, treaty

But Menelaus said, "Do not trouble yourself, my brother, for the wound is not deep." With their agreement broken by the **treacherous** act of Pandarus, both sides resumed their fierce fighting. And on both sides, the gods urged them on.

treacherous: not trustworthy; marked by deceit or betrayal

How Hector Bade Farewell to Andromache

With Ares, the god of war, at his side, Hector dealt death and destruction through the ranks of the Greeks. Hera and Athena saw him and were angered. They passed down to earth and helped

ATHENA HELPS THE GREEKS DRIVE BACK THE TROJANS.

the Greeks, who proceeded to drive back the Trojans.

After much fighting, Hector went to the city to tell the mothers of Troy to gather in the temple of Athena and pray to the goddess to calm her anger. Andromache, the wife of Hector, saw him and hurried to meet him. With her was a nurse carrying Hector's only child, with his golden hair shining like a star.

Andromache clasped Hector's hand and wept, saying, "Oh, Hector, your courage will bring you to death. If I lose you, then it would be better for me to die than to live. My father and my seven brothers all fell by the hand of the great Achilles. My dear mother, too, is dead. Have pity, then, and stay here. Do not leave me a widow, and your child an orphan."

But Hector said, "Dear wife, I am not willing that any son or daughter of Troy should see me stay away from battle. I hate the thought of it. I must make haste to return to my countrymen."

Then Hector stretched out his arms to his child. But the child drew back in the arms of his nurse with a loud cry, fearing the shining bronze

Hector takes leave of his wife Andromache.

armor and the horsehair that nodded from his helmet top. Father and mother both laughed aloud. And Hector took the helmet from his head and laid it on the ground, and caught the child in his hands and kissed him.

Hector prayed aloud: "Father Zeus and all ye gods, grant that this child may be great among the sons of Troy. And some day, when they see him carrying home the spoils of war, may they say, 'He is even greater than his father.'"

Then he gave the boy to his mother. She clasped him to her and smiled, but there were tears in her eyes. And Hector's heart was moved.

"Do not let these things trouble you," he said. "No man will kill me unless it is my fate to die. But no man, whether brave or cowardly, may escape fate."

Then Hector took up his helmet from the ground and put it on his head. Andromache returned to her home, often turning back her eyes to look at her husband, for in her heart she thought that she would never see him coming home again.

Hector went into battle with renewed strength, and everywhere the Greeks fell before him.

The Battle on the Plain

On a later day, the two armies again clashed on the open plain between the walls of Troy and the line of Greek ships near the shore. In the sky, Zeus held out his golden scales. In one scale he placed a weight for the Trojans and in the other a weight for the Greeks. The weights were weights of death, and the army whose weight was the heavier would suffer most on that day. And the scale of the Greeks sank lower. Then Zeus sent a thunderbolt into the army of the Greeks, and there was great fear among both men and horses.

The Greeks fled back to the barrier they had built to defend their ships. Hector drove them before him. As a dog follows a wild beast and catches him by the thigh as he flies, so did Hector follow the Greeks.

On the top of Olympus, Hera said to Athena, "I fear the Greeks will perish altogether by the hand of Hector."

Athena answered, "Make your chariot ready. We will go together to the battle, and Hector will not be glad when he sees us coming."

So Hera made her chariot ready, while Athena put on her armor and clasped her great spear. From high Olympus they **descended** towards Troy.

descended: went down

But Zeus saw them and called to Iris, the messenger of the gods, telling her, "Go now, Iris, and tell these two that they had better not set themselves against me. If they do, then I will lame their horses and break their chariot in pieces. If I strike them with a single thunderbolt, they will not recover from their hurts for ten years and more."

So Iris hurried and met the two goddesses on their way, and gave them the message of Zeus. When Hera heard it, she said to Athena, "It is not wise for us to fight with Zeus for the sake of men." So they went back to Olympus and sat down in their chairs of gold among the other gods, both very sad and angry.

Then Zeus came into the hall where the gods were assembled. When he saw Hera and Athena sitting by themselves with **gloomy** faces, he said, "Why do you look so sad? You know that what I choose to happen will happen. Even if all the other gods should

gloomy: unhappy, low-spirited

join together against me, still I shall **prevail** over them."

> **prevail:** prove more powerful; conquer

Athena, whose heart was bursting with anger, said nothing. But Hera said, "We know very well that you are stronger than all the gods. Still, we cannot help but pity the Greeks when we see them perishing in this way."

Zeus spoke again. "Do you pity the Greeks for what they have suffered? There is worse to come. For Hector will not cease driving the Greeks before him and slaying them till the great Achilles himself shall be moved to rise from the place where he sits by his ships."

And now the sun sank into the sea, and the night fell. The Trojans were angry that the darkness had come, but the Greeks were glad of the night, for it gave them time to breathe.

Then Hector called the Trojans to an assembly at a place near the river. He stood in the middle of the people, holding in his hand a spear sixteen feet or more in length, with a shining head of **bronze**. To the gathered people he said:

> **bronze:** a metal made of copper and tin

"Listen, men of Troy, and you allies who have

come to help us. I thought that today we would destroy the army of the Greeks and burn their ships. But night has come and prevented us from finishing our work. So let us sit down and rest and take a meal. Let us gather fuel so that we may burn fires all the night, and keep watch to see whether the Greeks try to **flee** in the night. Truly, they shall not go in peace. Tomorrow we will arm ourselves and drive these Greeks to their ships, and burn these ships with fire. Tomorrow shall surely bring ruin on the Greeks."

> **flee:** escape

So Hector spoke, and all the Trojans shouted with joy to hear such words. And, just as on a calm night the stars shine bright, so shone the thousand watch-fires of the Trojans as they waited for the morning.

The Ambassadors to Achilles

The Greek leaders gathered for a **council** of war. Agamemnon advised that they should take to their ships and set sail for Greece. "It seems," said the discouraged king, "to be the will

> **council:** a meeting of a group of people to discuss and decide issues

of Zeus that we shall never capture Troy."

Upon hearing this, the chiefs sat for a time in gloomy silence. Then brave Diomedes, king of Argos, spoke out.

"Do not be angry," said Diomedes to Agamemnon, "if I say that this talk of yours about fleeing in our ships is madness. Zeus has given you high rank and great power, but not much courage — and courage is the best gift of all. Return home if you want to, but we will stay until we have taken the city of Troy. We will not go back till we have done the thing we came to do."

These words were loudly applauded by the assembled leaders. Then wise old Nestor spoke:

"King Agamemnon, Zeus has made you lord over many nations. Therefore you have the greater need of good advice, even though it may not please you. It was an evil day when you sent the officers to take away Briseis from Achilles. The other chiefs did not agree to your deed, and I myself advised you not to do it, but you followed your own pride and shamed the bravest of your followers. Now, therefore, undo this evil deed, and make peace with this man whom you have wronged."

Agamemnon stood up and said, "You have spoken true words, old sir. Truly I acted as a fool that day; I do not deny it. For not only is Achilles a great warrior but he is also dear to Zeus—and surely it is Zeus's will that we are put to flight so long as Achilles stands aside from the battle. And now, as I did him wrong, so I will **make amends**, giving him many times more than that which I took from him."

> **make amends:** pay back for a loss, make up for a wrong

The Greek chiefs were very glad to hear these words. They **resolved** to appoint ambassadors to send to Achilles to beg him to accept the gifts and make peace with Agamemnon. They chose for this mission an aged chief named Phoenix, who had taught Achilles in his youth. They also chose the valiant warrior Ajax Telamon, as well as swift-thinking Odysseus. The three ambassadors set out along the shore of the sea, and soon they found Achilles sitting in his tent with his friend Patroclus.

> **resolved:** decided on a course of action

Achilles warmly welcomed the three ambassadors as friends. Then wine was brought in, and after they had refreshed themselves, Odysseus stated the object of their visit. He described the dangers faced by the Grecian army, threatened with destruction by the terrible Hector and his allies. He told of the many gifts that Agamemnon offered, and urged Achilles to lay aside his anger and come to the aid of the Greeks.

"For truly," Odysseus concluded, "our need is great. Hector vows that he will burn our ships with fire and destroy us all. Take the gifts Agamemnon has offered. And if you do not care for Agamemnon, yet think of the people who perish because you stand aside from the battle. Take the gifts, for by so doing you will have wealth and honor and love from the Greeks, and great glory also, for you will slay Hector. He is ready to meet you in battle, for he is proud and thinks there is none among the Greeks who can stand against him."

Achilles answered, "I will speak plainly, Odysseus, and say what is in my heart—because to me, a man who thinks one thing in his heart but says another thing with his tongue is hateful as death itself. Tell me now, what good is it for a man to be always fighting day after day? I took many cities, and from all I carried away great riches. All this I brought to King Agamemnon, and he gave a few things to me and others, but kept most for himself. And then what did he do? He let the other chiefs keep what he had given them, but what he had given me, he took away. So to him I say, do not ask me to fight against the Trojans. There are other chiefs whom he has not wronged and shamed; let him go to them. As for Hector or any of the sons of Troy, I will not fight them again. Tomorrow, you will see my ships upon the sea, and my men rowing with all their might, back to our dear country, if the god of the sea is willing."

Achilles paused in his speech. Then he continued in a thoughtful tone:

"Long ago, my mother, Thetis of the sea, said to me, 'My son, two paths lie before you, and you may choose which you will follow. If you stay in this land and fight against Troy, then you will never go back to your own land but will die in your youth. Only your name will live forever. But if you will leave this land and go back to your home, then you shall live long, even to old age, but your name will be forgotten.' Once I thought that fame was a better thing than life. But now my mind is changed, for indeed my fame is taken from me, since Agamemnon has put me to shame before all the people."

Then old Phoenix stood up and spoke. "Achilles," he said, "Peleus, your father, made me your teacher. Now, I **pray you**, listen to me. Put away the anger in your heart. If, indeed, King Agamemnon had offered you no gifts, nor restored to you that which he took from you, then I would not ask you to cease from your anger. But now he gives you many gifts, and promises you yet more. Take the gifts that Agamemnon gives you. So shall all the Greeks honor you."

> **pray you:** beg you

Achilles answered, "Phoenix, good old man, trouble me no more with prayers and tears while you seek to help Agamemnon."

Ajax rose and said, "Let us go. We shall do no good here today. Achilles cares only for his anger and nothing for his comrades or his people. Surely he seems to lack reason."

Achilles answered, "You speak well, great Ajax. Indeed, the anger is still hot in my heart, because Agamemnon put me to shame before all the people. Go and tell him that I will not arise to do battle with the Trojans till Hector comes to these tents and seeks to set fire to my ships. If that happens, I will arise, and I will stop him."

So the ambassadors left to give the message of Achilles to King Agamemnon.

The Wounding of Hector and the Battle at the Ships

The next morning, as soon as it was light, Agamemnon led the Greeks into battle, and Hector led the Trojans.

The first man to break through the Trojan line was King Agamemnon. He drove the Trojans back to the walls of the city. Hector himself did not dare to stand up before him, for Iris had brought him this message from Zeus: "So long as Agamemnon fights in the front, hold back, for on this day he will win great honor for himself. But when he is wounded, then you will have the strength to drive the Greeks back to their ships."

Two Trojan warriors who were brothers

drove their chariot straight at Agamemnon. The king threw his spear at the younger of the two, but missed. Then the younger Trojan thrust at Agamemnon with his spear, driving it against his breastplate. The king caught the spear in his hand and drove it through the neck of the young warrior so that he fell dead from the chariot.

When the **elder** brother saw this, he thrust his spear at Agamemnon and pierced his arm beneath the elbow. Agamemnon, though wounded, fought back and killed the elder brother. The king continued to fight for a while, but when his arm grew cold and stiff, he said to his charioteer, "Now take me back to the ships, for I cannot fight any more."

Now the Trojans advanced, led by Hector, whose eyes flashed with fire.

When Poseidon, the god of the sea, saw the Greeks pushed back to their ships, he was troubled, for he loved the Greeks. Although Zeus had not allowed any god to help the Greeks, Poseidon saw that Zeus had his eyes turned from the battle. So Poseidon mounted his chariot and he passed over the waves, while the great beasts

elder: older

of the sea—whales and porpoises—sported about him.

POSEIDON

When Poseidon came to the land where the battle raged, he disguised himself as Calchas the soothsayer. He went among the Greeks and filled them with fresh strength, and they returned to the battle with new courage, driving back the Trojans.

Even great Hector himself was struck down for a time. He cast his spear at mighty Ajax

Telamon, but the point did not pierce the giant's thick, strong armor. As Hector turned to go back to his comrades, Ajax lifted a huge stone and threw it at Hector, hitting him on the neck.

Hector fell as an oak falls when the lightning has struck it. When they saw him drop, the Greeks rushed forward to drag away his body, but the Trojans lifted him from the ground and carried him away to the river.

When the Greeks saw that Hector was carried out of the battle, they took fresh courage and charged the Trojans. Zeus, who had turned his eyes again to the land of Troy, observed the Trojans fleeing, and Hector lying like one that has fallen in battle. In fury, Zeus cried out to Hera, "Is this your doing, **rebellious** one? Tell me the truth!"

rebellious: refusing to obey

And Hera answered, "No—it is Poseidon who gives the Greeks strength and courage."

Zeus sent Iris the messenger to deliver his angry command to Poseidon: "Go back to the sea and do not **meddle** with these affairs on earth!" Poseidon complained bitterly, but he obeyed.

meddle: interfere

Then Zeus told Apollo, "Go to Hector, where he lies like a dead man on the plain. Put new life and courage into him, and send him back to the battle with new strength."

Apollo hastened to Hector where he lay by the riverside, and said, "Hector, why do you take no part in the battle?"

Hector answered, "Is this a god that speaks to me? Did you not see how Ajax struck me down with a great stone, so that I could fight no more? Truly, I thought that I had gone down to the place of the dead."

"Take courage, my friend," replied Apollo. "Zeus has sent me to stand by you and help you. Call the Trojans together again, and lead them to the ships, and I will be with you."

Then Hector stood up, and his strength returned to him. He called to the Trojans and led them toward the Greeks.

The Greeks were amazed when they saw him, for they thought that his wounds meant certain death. Seeing Hector, they were struck with fear, like men who hunt a **stag** or a wild goat and find a lion instead.

stag: a male deer

And still Hector came on, and Apollo went before him, a cloud of fire round his shoulders, holding the great shield of Zeus in his hand. Many of the Greeks were slain that day. And the Trojans advanced as far as the Greek ships, Hector first of all. Close behind Hector was a chief who carried a torch in his hand, with which he aimed to set fire to a ship—but Ajax thrust his sword through his breast and killed him.

Hector cried, "Come on, men of Troy, for Zeus is with us. Even if a man die, it is a noble thing to die fighting for his country. His wife and children shall live in peace, and he himself shall be famous forever."

Thus did Hector urge his people to battle, and the Greeks fell back before them. And Hector cried, "Bring me fire that we may burn the ships of these robbers!"

On the deck of a Greek ship, Ajax fought bravely, thrusting at any one who came near with fire. As Ajax thrust at the Trojans with his spear, he cried to the Greeks with a terrible voice, saying, "Now you must fight like men! You are in the plain of Troy, and the sea is close behind us, and we are far from our own country. All our hope, therefore, is in courage, for there is no one to save you if you will not save yourselves!"

The Trojans attacked more fiercely than before, so that Ajax himself was forced to give way when Hector cut his spear shaft in two by a stroke of his huge sword. Then the Trojans hurled their blazing torches, and the ship was soon wrapped in flames.

How Patroclus Went into Battle

Achilles was standing on the stern of his ship, looking at the battle, when his companion Patroclus ran to him with bitter tears.

And Achilles said to him, "Patroclus, why do you weep like a child crying to be taken up into its mother's arms? Are you weeping for the Greeks because they perish for the **folly** of their king?"

folly: foolishness; lack of good sense

"Do not be angry with me, Achilles," said Patroclus, "for the Greeks are in deep trouble. If you will not go to battle, let me go, and let your warriors, the Myrmidons, go with me. Let me put on your armor—this will scare the Trojans, for they will think you have come back to the battle, and the Greeks will have time to rest."

Achilles answered, "I said that I would not fight again till the Trojans bring the fire near to my own ships. But I can see it is time to give help, for the Trojans are gathered about the ships, and the Greeks are pushed by their enemies almost to the sea. You may put on my armor and lead my people to the fight. Go, Patroclus, and keep the fire from the ships."

Patroclus turned to leave but Achilles stopped him and said, "When you have done this, come back and fight no more. Do not go not near the wall of Troy, for one of the gods may meet you there and harm you. For the Trojans are loved by the gods, especially the great archer Apollo with his deadly bow."

So Patroclus put on the armor of Achilles— breastplate and shield and helmet. Then he mounted the chariot drawn by the mighty horses of Achilles.

Meanwhile Achilles called his soldiers to battle. He had brought fifty ships to Troy, and in each there were fifty men. To them he cried out, "You complained that I kept you from the battle against your will. Now you have your wish."

So the Myrmidons went to battle, helmet to helmet and shield to shield, close as the stones with which a builder makes a wall. And Patroclus, in the armor of Achilles, went in front.

Then Achilles said, "O Zeus, father of all the gods, I send my comrade to this battle. Make him strong and bold, and give him glory, and bring him home safe to the ships, and my people with him."

So he prayed. Zeus heard his prayer, and part of it Zeus **granted**, but part of it he **denied**.

> **granted:** agreed to, allowed
> **denied:** refused

Patroclus approached a Greek ship that the Trojans had set on fire. When the Trojans saw him and the armor he wore, they ran, for they thought that Achilles had put aside his anger and come forth to fight. In his chariot, pulled by the swift and nimble horses of Achilles, Patroclus drove back and forth, slaying the Trojans as they sought to flee to their city.

Patroclus focused all of his attention on slaying Hector. He had forgotten Achilles' command that when he had saved the ships from fire, he should not fight any more.

Apollo stirred up the spirit of Hector to go against Patroclus. Hector ordered his charioteer, "We will see whether we cannot drive back this Patroclus, for it must be he—Achilles he is not, though he wears his armor."

When Patroclus saw them coming, he took a great stone from the ground and flung it at them. The stone struck the charioteer full on the helmet. As the man fell head foremost from the chariot, Patroclus shouted, "See how well he dives! Who would have thought that there should be such skillful divers in Troy?"

Three times Patroclus rushed against the men of Troy. But the fourth time Apollo stood behind him and struck him on the head so that his eyes grew dim. His helmet fell to the ground, and the horsehair plume was soiled with dust. Never before had it touched the ground, from the first day when Achilles wore it. The spear that Patroclus carried fell, broken, from his hand, and the shield fell from his arm. As he stood confused, Hector thrust at him with his spear, and he fell to the ground. And when the Greeks saw him fall they sent up a terrible cry.

Hector stood over him and cried, "Did you think you would destroy our city, Patroclus? Instead, you are slain, and the great Achilles cannot help you."

But Patroclus answered, "You boast too much, Hector. It was not you that slew me, but Apollo. And death is very close to you, for the great Achilles will slay you."

Hector answered, "Why do you **prophesy** death for me? It may be that the great Achilles himself will fall by my hand."

prophesy: predict

But Patroclus was already dead.

The Rousing of Achilles

Hector stripped off the armor from Patroclus — the armor that Achilles had given him to wear. Hector took off his own armor and put on himself the armor of Achilles. But when Hector began to drag away the body, Ajax Telamon came forward and put his big shield before it. As a lioness stands before its cubs and will not allow the hunter to take them, so did Ajax stand before the body of Patroclus and defend it from the Trojans.

As the fighting raged over the body of Patroclus, the horses of Achilles stood apart, and the tears fell from their eyes, for they loved Patroclus, and they knew that he was dead. The charioteer could not move them—the horses would neither enter the battle nor turn back to the ships. They stood with their heads drooped to the ground, the tears falling from their eyes, and their long manes trailing in the dust.

When Zeus saw them he pitied them in his heart, for these were immortal horses that the king of the gods had given to Achilles. And Zeus said, "I should not have given you immortal creatures to a mortal man, for of all things that live and move upon the earth, surely man is the most miserable. But Hector shall not have you. It is enough— indeed, it is too much—that he should have the arms of Achilles."

Then the horses moved from their place and obeyed the driver as before. And Hector could not take them, though he greatly desired so to do.

By this time a messenger had made his way to Achilles, weeping as he said, "I bring bad news. The men of Troy have the victory today. Patroclus lies dead, and Hector wears your armor."

Achilles took some of the dust of the plain in his hands and poured it on his head. He wept and tore his hair. His mother, Thetis, goddess of the sea, heard his cry and came and laid her hand on his head and asked, "Why do you weep, my son?"

Achilles answered, "My friend Patroclus is dead, and the arms I gave him to wear are now worn by Hector. I do not care to live, unless I can **avenge** his death!"

> **avenge:** to get back at someone; to punish someone for an injury done to you

Then Thetis said, "Be it so, my son. But you cannot go into battle without arms. Tomorrow I will furnish you with new armor."

While they talked the men of Troy drove the Greeks back more and more. Zeus sent his messenger Iris to Achilles.

"**Rouse** yourself, Achilles," said Iris, "or the body of Patroclus will be prey for the dogs of Troy."

> **rouse:** awaken; move from inaction to action

Achilles answered, "How shall I go? I have no armor."

Iris replied, "Go to the ships and show yourself. The Trojans will draw back, and the Greeks will have a breathing space."

So Achilles went. And Athena put her shield upon him and a golden halo above his head, making it shine as a flame. The men of Troy were astonished when they saw above his head the flaming fire that Athena had lit. He shouted aloud, and his voice was like a battle trumpet. The hearts of the men of Troy were filled with fear, and they fell back.

Then the Greeks took up the body of Patroclus and carried it to the tent of Achilles, and Achilles himself walked by its side, weeping. This had been a sad day, and to bring it sooner to an end, Hera commanded the sun to set before its time.

There was great **mourning** for Patroclus in the camp of the Greeks. They washed his body and put **ointment** into the wounds. Then they laid the body on a bed, and covered it with a linen cloth from the head to

mourning: expressions of sorrow for someone who has died

ointment: an oily substance used to heal or soothe

the feet, and over the cloth they put a white robe.

And Achilles vowed, "I will not bury Patroclus till I can bring the head and the armor of Hector to honor him."

The Making of the Arms

Thetis, immortal mother of Achilles, went to the house of Hephaestus, the god of all who work in gold and silver and iron. He was busy at his **forge**, making **cauldrons** for the palace of the gods.

forge: a furnace for melting metal; also, a blacksmith's workshop

cauldrons: large metal pots (for cooking over an open fire)

The wife of Hephaestus greeted Thetis, saying, "O goddess whom we love and honor, what brings you here? Gladly will we serve you." To her husband she called out, "Thetis is here. Come quickly."

Hephaestus answered, "No guest could be more welcome to me than Thetis. When my mother made me leave her house because I was lame, Thetis and her sister received me in their house under the sea. Nine years I dwelt there, and hammered many a **trinket** for

trinket: small piece of jewelry

them in a hollow cave that was close by. I would give my life to serve Thetis."

Then he came in and assured Thetis, "Tell me all that is in your mind, for I will do whatever you ask, if it can be done."

Thetis told him how Patroclus had been slain in battle, and how the armor of Achilles was lost. "I **pray** you," she said, "make new armor for my son—a shield, and a helmet, and greaves for his legs, and a breastplate."

pray: ask, urge, beg

Hephaestus answered, "I will make for him such arms as men will wonder at when they see them."

So he went to his forge and turned the **bellows** to the fire. He put copper and tin and gold and silver into the fire until they had softened, and then took the hammer in one hand and the **tongs** in the other.

bellows: a tool with an air bag, that, when squeezed, blows air onto a fire

tongs: a tool with long arms, used to pick up and hold things

First he made a shield, great and strong, with a silver belt with which to grip it. On it he fashioned an image of the earth and the sky and the sea, with the sun and the moon and all the stars. Also he made images of two cities—in one city there was peace, and in the other city there was war.

Also he created an image of one field in which men were plowing, and of another in which **reapers** reaped the corn. Behind the reapers came boys who gathered the corn in their arms and bound it. And round about the shield he made the ocean, like a great river.

> **reapers:** workers who harvest a crop

Also he made a breastplate, and a great helmet with a ridge of gold, and greaves of tin for the legs. When he had finished all his work, he gave the shield and the other pieces to Thetis. She flew, swift as a hawk, to where her son stayed by the ships. She found him lying on the ground, holding in his arms the body of Patroclus, weeping aloud while his men **lamented**.

> **lamented:** expressed sadness and grief

The goddess took her son by the hand and said, "It was the will of the gods that he should die. But you must think about other things. Take this gift from Hephaestus, beautiful armor such as man has never yet worn."

She placed the armor at the feet of Achilles. It shone so brightly that the eyes of the Myrmidons were dazzled by it. Achilles took up the arms, glad at heart to see them, and said, "Mother, these are truly arms that could only be made by a god. Gladly will I put them on for the battle."

Then Achilles marched by the ships, shouting to the Greeks to prepare for battle. And they all came, ready to fight. The chiefs gathered in assembly, including Odysseus and King Agamemnon, who leaned on their spears because their wounds were fresh.

Achilles spoke: "It was a foolish thing, King Agamemnon, about which we quarreled. But let us put all that behind us. Here I make an end of my anger. Make haste, then, and call the Greeks to battle."

Then King Agamemnon answered, "Listen, all you Greeks. You have blamed me for this quarrel. Yet it was not I, but the **Fury** who turns the thoughts of men to madness, that brought it about. Still, it is for me to make amends. Achilles, I will give you all the gifts that Odysseus promised in my name. Stay here till my people bring these treasures from the ships."

> **Fury:** one of the Furies, three goddesses of vengeance in Greek mythology

Achilles said, "You may give the gifts, or keep them for yourself. There is only one thing I care for—to get to the battle without delay."

Then Odysseus said, "Let us take a meal first, for the battle will be long, and a man who has not eaten cannot fight from morning to sunset. Let us strengthen ourselves that we may fight the better."

Achilles replied, "How can I think of feasting when Patroclus lies dead? I will not eat or drink till I have had vengeance."

And so the Greeks took their meal, but Achilles sat apart, refusing to eat.

In high Olympus, Zeus said to Athena, "Do you not care for your dear Achilles? See how the other Greeks eat and drink, but he sits apart."

So Athena flew down from Olympus and poured heavenly food into Achilles. He did not know what she did, but he felt the new strength inside him. Then he armed himself with the arms that Thetis had brought from Hephaestus, and he took from its case the great spear which no man but he could **wield**.

wield: to hold and use (a weapon or tool)

After this he climbed into his chariot, and he said to his horses, "Take care now, Xanthus and

Balius that you do not leave your master today, as you left Patroclus yesterday, dead on the field."

Then Hera gave a voice to the horse Xanthus, and he said, "It was not our fault, Achilles, that Patroclus died. It was Apollo who slew him, but Hector had the glory. You too, some day, shall be slain by a god and a man."

Achilles answered, "I know my fate, but I do not care so long as I may have vengeance on the Trojans."

How Achilles Avenged the Death of Patroclus

Achilles gathered the Greeks for the battle. The Trojans, too, had assembled on the wide plain between their city walls and the shore.

Then Achilles rushed into the battle, slaying as he went. Hector would have met him, but Apollo said to him, "Do not fight with Achilles, for he is stronger than you and will slay you." But when Hector saw his youngest brother slain before his eyes, he could bear it no longer and rushed to meet Achilles.

ACHILLES RUSHED INTO THE BATTLE, SLAYING AS HE WENT.

When Achilles saw Hector, he said to himself, "The time has come; this is the man who killed Patroclus." And to Hector he said, "Come and taste of death."

Hector answered, "One man may be stronger than another, but it is Zeus who gives the victory."

Achilles leapt at Hector with a shout, but Apollo snatched him away. Three times did Achilles leap at him, and three times he struck only the dust. The fourth time he cried with a terrible voice, "Dog, these four times you have escaped from death, but I shall meet you again when Apollo is not at hand to help you."

Now Achilles turned to the ranks of the Trojans and slew many of them. But Apollo came to the aid of the Trojans by drawing Achilles away from the city. Apollo took the form of a Trojan chief, and Achilles followed him far from the walls of Troy. At last the god turned and said, "Why do you follow me, swift-footed Achilles? Have you not yet discovered that I am a god, and all your **fury** is **in vain**?"

fury: anger

in vain: useless, unsuccessful, without value

In great wrath Achilles cried, "Apollo, you have done me wrong in drawing me away from the city." And he turned and rushed back toward the walls of Troy.

The Trojans were now safe in their city. Hector alone remained outside the walls, standing in front of the gates. King Priam called out to Hector, urging his son to come within the walls. Then Hector's mother, Queen Hecuba, called to him. She wept aloud, saying, "O Hector, my son, I beg you, come inside the wall. Do not stand up in battle against Achilles."

But her **appeals** were in vain, for Hector was resolved to await the coming of Achilles. And as he waited many thoughts passed through his mind.

appeals: urgent requests

"It is better," thought Hector, "for me to stay here and meet the great Achilles, and either slay him, or, if it must be so, be slain by him. Or shall I lay down my shield and take off my helmet and lean my spear against the wall, and go meet him and say, 'We will give back the fair Helen and all the riches that Paris carried off with her, as well as all the riches in the city, if only you will leave us in peace'? But this is **idle** talk. He will have no pity, and will slay me as I stand before him. No—it is far better to meet in arms and see whether Zeus will give the victory to him or to me."

idle: pointless

These were the things that Hector thought in his heart as Achilles drew near, his armor flashing like the blaze of the sun when it rises.

Hector trembled when he saw him, and his heart failed him so that he turned and fled. Fast he ran from the gates, and fast Achilles **pursued** him. Past the watchtower they ran, past the wind-blown fig tree, along the wagon-road that went about the walls. And all the gods looked on from their home on Mount Olympus.

pursued: chased; followed after in order to catch

And Zeus said, "This is a **piteous** thing I see. My heart **grieves** for Hector—Hector, who has never failed to honor me and the other gods with sacrifice. See how the great Achilles is pursuing him! Shall we save him from death, or shall we let him fall by the spear of Achilles?"

piteous: sad, pitiful, heartbreaking

grieves: feels deep sadness and distress

Athena said, "Will you save a man whom fate has **appointed** to die? Do this, if you will, but the other gods do not approve."

appointed: decided on a time or place

Then said Zeus, "This is a thing I hate. But be it as you will."

Just as in a dream, when one seems to flee and another seems to pursue, and the first cannot escape, but neither can the second overtake, so Hector and Achilles ran. All this time Apollo helped Hector, or he could not have escaped Achilles, who was the swiftest of men.

Three times did they run round the city, but when they came for the fourth time, Zeus on Mount Olympus held out the golden scales of fate. In one scale he put the fate of Achilles, and in the other the fate of Hector—and the scale of Hector sank down. Immediately Apollo departed from the field, for he could no longer defy fate.

Achilles now drew near to Hector and threw his spear, but Hector saw it coming and crouched on the ground, so that it flew above his head and fixed itself in the earth. Unseen by Hector, Athena snatched the spear and gave it back to Achilles.

Hector now launched his spear. With true aim he hurled it, for it struck the very middle of Achilles' shield. But the shield made by a god could not be pierced by a mortal weapon, and so the spear of Hector fell to the ground.

Hector then he knew that his end had come. He said to himself, "Zeus and Apollo are with me no longer, but if I must die, let me at least die doing a deed that men shall remember in the years to come."

He drew his mighty sword and rushed at Achilles as an eagle rushes down from the clouds upon its prey. But Achilles charged to meet him, the gleam of his spear-point as bright as the evening star. Achilles well knew the one unprotected spot in the armor that Hector had taken from Patroclus. Into the spot where the neck joins the shoulder he drove his spear, and Hector fell in the dust.

With his last breaths, Hector asked Achilles to return his body to Troy for a proper burial. And he spoke this warning: "Achilles, beware the anger of the gods. The day will come when Paris, with the help of Apollo, will slay you here by these gates." So died the great champion of the Trojans.

"Lie there in death," said Achilles, "and I will meet my own when it pleases the gods to send it." Then he drew his spear out of Hector's body and stripped off the bloody armor. But his wrath was not calmed even by the death of his foe. He tied the feet of the fallen Hector with cords of leather to the back of his chariot, leaving the head to trail along the ground. And Achilles drove to the ships, dragging the dead hero in the dust.

The Trojans, beholding this **dreadful** sight from the walls of the city, broke out into loud cries of grief. Andromache, the wife of

dreadful: causing great fear or sadness

Hector, had not seen the combat between the two heroes. She was at home with her **handmaidens**, preparing for Hector's return from the battle. But when she heard the loud wails, she rose in great fear and called to her handmaidens. "Come with me," she cried, "for I fear that some evil has come to the Trojans."

handmaidens: female servants

Andromache faints into the arms of her handmaidens.

She went up to the tower and, looking out on the plain, saw the body of her beloved Hector dragged behind the wheels of the chariot of Achilles. Overpowered at the sight, she sank fainting into the arms of her handmaidens.

While the Trojans mourned the loss of Hector, the Greeks made preparations for funeral services in honor of Patroclus. The ceremonies lasted three days. Many trees were cut down on Mount Ida and carried to the plain, where the logs were heaped together in an immense pile, a hundred feet square. Upon this they placed the body of Patroclus. Achilles cut off a lock of his own hair and put it in the dead hero's hand, and each of the other warriors placed a lock of his hair on the body.

Torches were now applied, and all through the night the pile blazed with a mighty roar. In the morning, the bones of Patroclus were gathered up and enclosed in a golden **urn**. On the spot where the **pyre** had stood they raised a mound of earth as a monument to the hero.

urn: a vase used to store the remains of a cremated person

pyre: a fire for burning a dead body in a funeral ceremony

Then, as was the custom, there were funeral games, athletic competitions among the Greek heroes, with the winners receiving valuable prizes given by Achilles—prizes of gold and silver, and shining weapons, and steeds, and oxen. There were chariot races, wrestling matches, and contests with swords and with bows and arrows.

Thus did Achilles honor his dead friend with funeral **rites** and funeral games. But his wrath against Hector continued, even when he had dragged the hero's body with his chariot three times round the tomb of Patroclus. He repeated this cruel insult at dawn for several days. But Apollo watched over the body and protected it from harm.

> **rites:** rituals; religious ceremonies

Priam's Appeal to Achilles

Seeing how the body of Hector was shamefully treated, Zeus sent for Thetis and said to her, "Go to the camp, and tell your son to give up the body of Hector for **ransom**. It angers me to see him dishonor the dead."

> **ransom:** a payment made to free a captured person

So Thetis went to the tent of Achilles and found him weeping softly for his dead friend. And she said to him, "It is the will of Zeus that you give up the body of Hector for ransom."

And Achilles said, "If the gods will it, then so be it."

Then Zeus sent his messenger Iris to King Priam, where he sat in his palace with his sons and daughters weeping around him. Iris said to him, "Be of good cheer. Zeus **bids** you take precious gifts to buy back the body of Hector from Achilles."

> **bids:** commands, orders

Priam rose to go at once but his wife, Queen Hecuba, tried to keep him back, fearing for his life. But the old king said, "I have heard the voice of the messenger of Zeus, and I will go. And if I die, what do I care? Let Achilles slay me, so long as I hold the body of my son once more in my arms."

Then he had a wagon loaded with many treasures. Before he set off, he prayed: "Hear me, Father Zeus, and grant that Achilles may pity me. Send me a sign, in order that I may go with a good heart to the Greeks."

And Zeus sent an eagle, his favorite bird, as a

sure sign. Then the old man mounted his chariot and drove forth from the palace, while another man drove the wagon loaded with treasures.

As they crossed the plain they were met by the god Hermes, whom Zeus had sent to conduct them safely to the tent of Achilles. As they approached the tent, the god cast the guards into a deep sleep, so that the Trojan king and his companion were not seen by any of the Greeks.

When Priam reached the tent of Achilles, he stepped down from the chariot and went to the tent. The king fell on the ground before Achilles, clasped his knees, and spoke.

"Think of your father, Achilles, and pity me," said Priam. "Many valiant sons I had, and many have I lost. And now the best of them all is dead." Then Priam touched his lips to Achilles' hands and said, "I kiss the hands that killed my son."

Then the heart of Achilles was moved with pity and he wept, thinking of his own father and of the dead Patroclus. He stood up from his seat and said, "How did you dare to come to my tent, old man? Surely you must have a heart of iron. But come, sit and eat and drink."

But the king said, "Do not ask me to eat and drink while my son lies unburied and without honor. Rather, take the gifts that I have brought to ransom him."

Achilles frowned. At last he said, "I will give back the body of Hector." And Priam said nothing, for he feared to rouse the anger of Achilles.

Then Achilles went forth from the tent, and two companions with him. They removed the gifts from the wagon. Achilles ordered that the body of Hector be washed and **anointed**. And when this was done, Achilles himself lifted the body in his arms and put it in the wagon.

Then he went back to his tent and said to Priam, "Your son, old man, is ransomed, and tomorrow shall you see him and take him back to Troy."

They looked at each other—and Achilles wondered at King Priam, so noble was he to behold, and Priam wondered to see how strong and how fair was Achilles.

Then King Priam said, "If you are willing to let me bury Hector, let there be a truce between my people and the Greeks. For nine days let us mourn. On the tenth we will bury him, on the eleventh raise a great tomb above him, and on the twelfth we will fight again, if fight we must."

And Achilles answered, "Be it so."

Priam took the body back to the city of Troy. The king's daughter, Cassandra, stood watching on the high walls, and when she saw them coming, she cried out, "Sons and daughters of Troy, go to meet Hector, just as you once met him with joy as he came back in triumph from battle."

The people poured out onto the plain. Andromache led the way, followed by the queen and crowds of mourners. Last of all came Helen, who cried, "Many a year has passed since I came to Troy— would that I had died before! Never, Hector,

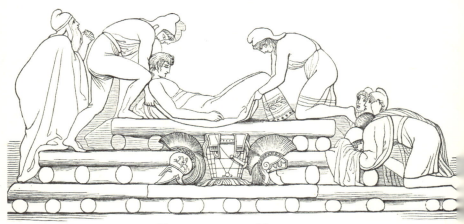

THE FUNERAL OF HECTOR

have I heard from your lips one bitter word. I weep for you, for now I have no friend in all of Troy. All **shun** and hate me now."

shun: purposefully avoid

For nine days the people of Troy gathered wood to build a great pyre. On the tenth they laid Hector upon the pile and kindled a fire beneath it. When the body was burned, his comrades gathered the bones and laid them in a chest of gold. This they covered with purple robes and put in a great coffin, and upon it they laid many great stones. Over all they raised a mighty mound.

Thus they buried Hector, defender of Troy.

AFTER THE *ILIAD*

With the funeral of Hector, the *Iliad* ends. In the beginning of the *Iliad*, in the invocation of the muse, the poet announced his great theme as the wrath of Achilles. And so the poem closes when the results of the hero's wrath have been told.

Other ancient myths, which are not part of the *Iliad*, tell the story of how Achilles met his fate, and how the Trojan War ended.

The Death of Achilles

After the funeral of Hector, the fighting began again. For a time the Trojans remained within the walls of their city, which were strong enough to resist all the enemy's attacks. But when allies arrived to help the Trojans, they came forth again to fight the Greeks on the open plain.

Among the allies of Troy were the famous female warriors known as Amazons, led by their bold queen, Penthesilea. She led her valiant band of woman warriors out through the gates and made a fierce attack on the Greeks. A great battle then began, and many warriors on both sides were laid in the dust.

Penthesilea herself was slain by Achilles. Achilles was at first unwilling to fight her, and he tried to avoid meeting the queen. But she attacked him furiously, first hurling her spear, and then rushing upon him sword in hand. Achilles fought back and **mortally** wounded her.

mortally: so seriously as to cause death

As the brave queen fell, she asked Achilles to permit her body to be taken away by her own people. Filled with admiration for her courage, Achilles granted the request.

The time soon came when Achilles—who so far had conquered in every fight—would meet his own doom.

There was a great battle in which the Greeks, led by Achilles, drove the Trojans back to the city walls. Through the great western gate, which lay open, the Trojans rushed in terror and confusion, with the Greeks pressing close behind.

Achilles reached the gate and was about to enter. But Paris aimed at him with an arrow.

Guided by Apollo, the arrow struck Achilles in the heel—the only part in which he could be fatally wounded. (His mother, you remember, had dipped the infant Achilles in the waters of the river Styx—and when she did so, she held him by the heel, so his heel alone remained untouched by the magic water, and therefore vulnerable.)

Some of the ancient stories say that the arrow shot by Paris was tipped with poison. Others say that when Achilles was struck by the arrow, he fell to the ground and was then killed by another arrow, or by a sword.

A fierce struggle took place over the body of Achilles, but by mighty efforts Ajax Telamon and Odysseus succeeded in gaining possession of it and carrying it to the Grecian camp. Deep was the grief of the Greeks at the death of their great champion. Magnificent funeral rites and games were celebrated in his honor, and a vast mound was raised on the shore as a monument to the fallen hero.

The Wooden Horse

The Greeks had now lost their most powerful warrior. They began to think that it might be impossible for them to take Troy by force, and that they must try other methods.

So the crafty Odysseus, inspired by Athena, thought of a plan to take the city. He guided the Greeks to build a huge and hollow wooden horse. When it was finished, dozens of Greek warriors climbed up and entered an opening in the belly of the wooden horse and hid inside. Then the opening was sealed and the rest of the Greeks broke up their camp, boarded their ships, and sailed away from Troy.

The people of Troy were very glad indeed, for it appeared that the Greeks had given up the siege and decided to return home. The Trojans opened the city gates, and men, women, and children hurried out to the plain where so many battles had been fought.

And there, standing on the plain, they saw the great wooden horse. One man said, "Let us drag it into the city to be a monument to all that we have suffered for the last ten years." Another cried, "No, let us burn it, or drag it down and plunge it into the sea." And one said, "Whatever it is, I fear the Greeks even when they give us gifts."

At this moment some shepherds approached, bringing with them a man whose hands were tied behind his back. He said that his name was Sinon, and that he was a Greek. His fellow Greeks, he said, had decided to give up the war, and also to offer one of themselves as a sacrifice to the gods, so that they might get fair winds for sailing home. When they selected him to be the victim, Sinon said, he fled and hid himself by the river, where the shepherds found him.

Then King Priam took pity on him and gave an order to unbind his hands. "Forget your own people," said the king to Sinon. "From this day on, you are one of us. But tell us why the Greeks made this great horse of wood."

Sinon lifted his hands and said, "O great King Priam, the wooden horse is an offering to Athena. The Greeks have made it so large to prevent the Trojans from dragging it through the gates into the city. For once within the city walls,

After the Iliad

it will bring safety to Troy and **woe** to the Greeks."

woe: great sadness, misery

So Sinon spoke, and the Trojans believed him. They put rollers under the feet of the horse, and fastened ropes to it, and dragged it through the great gate into the city. King Priam's daughter Cassandra warned them that it would bring ruin upon Troy, but no one believed her.

That night the Trojans celebrated, not knowing that the end of their city was close at hand. For the Greeks had only pretended to go away. In truth, they had sailed their ships away from Troy, but no farther than a little island close by. There they hid, ready to come back when the signal was given.

And late that night, they saw the signal, a burning torch. Quickly and quietly the Greeks rowed back to Troy. And Sinon—a spy whom the Greeks had left to **deceive** the Trojans—opened the door in the wooden horse and let out the warriors who were hidden inside.

deceive: to use falsehoods to make someone believe something

The Trojans, startled from their sleep by the noise, understood at once what had happened. Hastily they rushed to arm themselves. Led by

The Trojan Horse

Aeneas, second only to Hector in valor amongst the Trojans, they fought bravely to drive out the enemy. But it was too late.

The victorious Greeks swept through the city. Menelaus found his wife Helen. Persuaded by the goddess Aphrodite, he forgave her and took her with him to his ships.

The Fall of Troy

When old King Priam saw the enemy break into his palace, he put on his armor. He had not worn it for many years, but now he felt that he must fight.

As he took a spear in his hand, his wife, Queen Hecuba, who sat with her daughter and the wives of her sons, cried to him, "Why have you put on your armor? Come and sit with us. Here you will be safe, or at least we will die together."

So she made the old man sit down near her. And at that moment, their son, Polites, stumbled into the room, wounded by the spear of Pyrrhus, the son of Achilles. As Polites came within the sight of his father and mother, he fell dead upon the ground.

King Priam looked up at Pyrrhus, whose bronze armor was streaked with blood. Then Priam could hold back no longer. He rose and shouted at Pyrrhus, "Now may the gods punish you for this wickedness, you who have killed a son before the eyes of his father!" As he spoke, the old man cast a spear at Pyrrhus, but there was no strength in it. Then Pyrrhus drove his sword into old Priam's body.

The Greeks carried on their work of destruction. They carried off to their ships all the riches of Troy, and many women as captives. Then they set fire to the city, and in a few hours nothing remained of Troy but a mass of ruins.

A Later Epic of Rome
The Trojan prince Aeneas escaped from Troy with his family and a number of other people. After many adventures, Aeneas reached the land we now know as Italy. There he established a settlement, and it is said that his descendants were the founders of Rome. The story of Aeneas is told in the epic poem called the *Aeneid* (ih-**nee**-id), written by the Roman poet Virgil in the first century BCE.

SELECTIONS FROM THE *ODYSSEY*

*Tell me, O Muse, of that **ingenious** hero who, after he had **sacked** the city of Troy, wandered far and wide, and saw the cities of many people, and learned their ways. Many were the **woes** he suffered upon the sea, seeking to save his own life and bring his men safely home. O goddess, daughter of Zeus, tell me of these things.*

ingenious: clever, inventive, imaginative

sacked: raided and looted

woes: heavy troubles; great sadness

A Visit from a Goddess

In the halls of Olympus, the gods were gathered together—all but Poseidon, the sea god, who hated Odysseus and kept him from reaching his home after he and his men had sailed away from Troy.

> **Poseideon's Anger**
> In the *Iliad*, Poseidon favored the Greeks in their fight against Troy. So why does he now hate the Greek hero Odysseus? That will be explained later in the *Odyssey*.

THE GODS MEET IN COUNCIL ON MOUNT OLYMPUS.

Zeus, king of the gods, was first to speak. "See now," said Zeus, "how people blame us gods for their own **folly**."

folly: foolishness

Then Athena, daughter of Zeus and goddess of wisdom, replied, "For their foolish or evil actions, some men deserve their suffering. But my heart aches for Odysseus, when I think of how he suffers far away from all his friends and family. Father Zeus, why do you ignore poor Odysseus? Did he not offer you many gifts and sacrifices in the land of Troy? Why, then, are you so angry with him?"

And Zeus said, "My child, what are you talking about? How can I forget Odysseus?

Selections from the Odyssey

No man on earth is more capable or more generous in his offerings to the immortal gods. But Poseidon is still furious with Odysseus. And, while he will not go so far as to kill Odysseus, Poseidon **torments** him by preventing him from getting home. Still, let us work together to help Odysseus, for Poseidon will not be able to stand against us all."

> **torments:** causes emotional or physical pain

Athena said, "If the gods intend to help Odysseus reach his home, then I will go to **Ithaca** to stir up the spirit of Odysseus's son, Telemachus."

Athena grasped her bronze spear, and down she darted from the **summits** of Olympus to the island of Ithaca, where she appeared in **disguise** in front of Odysseus's house. Inside the house sat Telemachus, sad and **brooding**. Years ago, when Telemachus was a child only a month old, his father had been called to join the war against Troy.

> **Ithaca:** Odysseus's homeland, an island that is now part of Greece, located to the west of continental Greece
>
> **summits:** highest points of hills or mountains
>
> **disguise:** an appearance that conceals one's true identity
>
> **brooding:** thinking anxiously about unhappy matters

On that long-ago day, Odysseus reluctantly said goodbye to his infant son, his young wife

Penelope, and his father, old Laertes. He took his sailors and his fighting men with him and he sailed away from the island of Ithaca where he was king.

After ten years, Troy was at last taken by the kings and princes of Greece, but still Odysseus did not return. Ten years more went by, with no word of Odysseus. And now that infant son he had left behind, Telemachus, had grown up and was a young man.

On this day, as Telemachus sat in his father's house, he was surrounded by a busy troop of servants preparing for a great feast. Some were carrying platters of roast meat, others were filling huge bowls with wine and water, and others were washing the tables. In and around the house many young **nobles** lounged, relaxing on couches or playing games, to pass the time until the feast would be ready. Their talk was loud and rowdy, showing no respect for themselves or for others.

nobles: persons of high rank or royal status; people of wealth and power

A traveler approached the gateway that led into the **courtyard** of Odysseus's house. He was a man of middle age, carrying a long spear in his hand. Seeing

courtyard: an open area enclosed by the walls of a building or buildings

the stranger standing unnoticed at the entrance, Telemachus hurried towards him, his hand held out in welcome.

"Forgive me, friend," Telemachus said, "for not noticing you sooner. My thoughts were far away. But welcome to the house of Odysseus. Come inside and take some refreshment."

"I thank you," said the stranger, "and I am glad to enter the house of the **renowned** Odysseus."

renowned: widely known and honored

The stranger followed Telemachus into the great hall of the house and placed his spear in a stand. Telemachus led him to a corner, away from the noisy crowd of men. A handmaiden brought water in a golden pitcher and poured it over their hands into a basin of silver. A table was set before them, heaped with good things to eat. Then **host** and guest together comforted their hearts with food and wine.

host: one who receives and cares for others as guests

But now Telemachus and his guest were disturbed by the crowd of men who ate and drank and talked loudly. They stared rudely at the stranger.

Telemachus drew his chair closer to the stranger and said quietly, "You see these unwelcome men who are feasting and giving orders in my father's house. Once there was a man who would have driven them like frightened hounds from this hall. Sadly, his bones lie at the bottom of the sea. But, sir, now that you have eaten, tell me, who are you, and where is your home? Is this your first visit to Ithaca, or are you an old friend of this house?"

"My name is Mentes," answered the stranger, "and I am a prince of a brave race of sailors. I am a friend of this house, well known to its master, Odysseus, and his father, Laertes. But tell me now, are you not the son of Odysseus? I knew him well, and you have his face and eyes."

"Yes, I am his son," replied Telemachus.

"Now explain to me once more," said Mentes. "What is the meaning of this lawless **riot** in the house? What has brought all these men here?"

riot: great disturbances

"I will tell you," answered Telemachus. "These are the men who have come to **woo** my mother. They demand she choose one of them to marry. But she will give no answer to

woo: to try to win someone's affection

them, for she ever hopes for her husband's return. And while she keeps them waiting for her answer, they eat up my father's goods. Before long, I think, they will make an end of me as well."

"How I wish," said Mentes, "that Odysseus were here with his helmet, shield, and spears. He would soon deal with these suitors. It may or may not be the will of the gods that he return, but either way, you must get these men out of your house. Therefore, **take heed**, and do as I tell you."

> **take heed:** pay close attention; listen carefully

With his gray, clear, shining eyes, the stranger looked steadily at Telemachus and said, "Tomorrow call these suitors to the place of assembly, and there stand up and tell them that the time has come for them to depart to their homes. Then prepare a ship with twenty rowers to take you to Pylos, where old King Nestor dwells. He was with Odysseus in the war of Troy; ask him for news of your father. From Pylos go to Sparta, the kingdom of Menelaus, the last of the Greeks to reach home after the fall of Troy—perhaps from him you may learn some news of your father."

"Already," said Telemachus, "your gaze and

your speech make me feel equal to the task."

"If you learn that your renowned father is indeed dead and gone," continued the stranger, "then return home and hold a great funeral in his memory. And then may your mother choose a good man to be her husband, knowing that Odysseus will never come back. After that, you must punish those who have wasted your father's goods and insulted his house. You are a man now, and must play a man's part. And when you have done these things, Telemachus, you will rise to fame and be free to seek your own fortune. But now, I must proceed on my journey."

As he led the stranger from the hall to the outer gate, Telemachus said, "I will not forget what you have told me. I know you possess a wise and a friendly heart."

The stranger clasped the young man's hands and went through the gate. Then, as Telemachus looked after him, he saw the stranger change in form. First he became a woman, tall and fair-haired, with a spear of bronze in her hand. And then the woman changed into a great sea-eagle that rose on wide wings and flew high through the air. Telemachus knew then that his visitor was an immortal and no other than the goddess Athena, who had been his father's friend.

Telemachus Addresses the Suitors

Telemachus returned to the hall. As he passed through the crowd, one suitor turned to another and said, "Never before did I see Telemachus hold himself so proudly."

Some men called out for the **minstrel** to come and sing to amuse them. The minstrel came and sang a sad tale of the homecoming of the Greeks from Troy, and of how some god or goddess heaped troubles upon them as they left the ruined city.

> **minstrel:** in ancient times, one who sang songs and recited poetry

As the minstrel sang, Telemachus's mother, Penelope, came down the stairs with two **handmaidens** beside her. When she heard the words he sang, Penelope cried, "Oh, have you no other song to sing but this tale that fills my heart with tears?"

> **handmaidens:** female servants

"Mother," said Telemachus, "do not blame the minstrel for his song. He did not cause the sadness of which he sings. You must learn to **endure** that story, for long will it be sung, and far and wide. And many other men besides Odysseus were lost in the war of Troy."

> **endure:** to suffer some difficulty, to put up with some hardship

THE MINSTREL SINGS TO THE SUITORS OF PENELOPE.

Penelope looked in surprise at the youth who spoke to her so wisely. Was this indeed Telemachus, who before had hardly lifted his head? And as she looked at him again she saw that he carried his head high and proudly, so like his father. She saw that her son was now indeed a man.

Then Penelope felt the eyes of the suitors gazing at her. She heard them muttering to each other that she would soon have to choose one of them for her husband. She turned away and went up the steep stairs with her handmaidens. Soon she sat at her **loom**, with many thoughts stirring her mind, until Athena soothed her spirit with sweet sleep.

> **loom:** a machine for weaving yarn or thread into cloth

As Penelope left, the suitors began their usual noise, but Telemachus raised his voice and silenced them.

"**Wooers** of my mother," he said, "let us feast now in peace and listen to the tale that the minstrel sings, for it is a rare thing to hear a man with such a voice. But in the morning meet me in the assembly, where I will give you formal notice to leave this house. For if you keep up your wild and wasteful ways here, then by the will of Zeus, the day will come when you shall be defeated and no longer rule in my father's house, and there shall be no man to **avenge** you."

> **wooers:** suitors; those trying to win a woman in marriage
>
> **avenge:** to get back at someone; to punish someone for an injury done to you

The suitors wondered at the boldness of his speech. One said, "Now, hear the young **braggart**!" Then, as it was growing late, the suitors departed to their homes, and Telemachus went to his room to sleep.

braggart: someone who boasts and brags

Before him walked an aged woman, carrying a torch to light his way. This was Eurycleia, who loved him dearly, for she had been his **nurse** when he was a baby.

nurse: a person who cares for young children

Telemachus thought of what he would say at the assembly the next day, and on what the goddess Athena had told him to do, and on his coming journeys to Nestor in Pylos and to Menelaus in Sparta. All night he lay sleepless, wondering about the dangers that awaited him.

When **rosy-fingered** dawn appeared, Telemachus rose from his bed and dressed himself. He hung his sharp sword across his shoulder and took in his hand a spear of bronze. Then he went down to the place of assembly, and two swift hounds went beside him.

rosy-fingered: a descriptive phrase meaning streaked with pink and red

When he arrived he found the princes and elders of the people already gathered together.

Selections from the Odyssey

The oldest among them, Aegyptus, rose to speak.

"Never have we met together in **council** since the day when Odysseus set sail from Ithaca," said Aegyptus. "Why have we been brought together now? Is there news of the return of those who followed him to Troy? Or is it some other business that brings us here?"

council: a meeting of a group of people to discuss and decide issues

Telemachus was bursting with what he had to say. The **herald** put a **staff** into his hands as a sign that he was to be listened to with respect. Then Telemachus turned to Aegyptus and spoke.

herald: an official who made announcements on behalf of a king or governing body, whose staff was a symbol of his office

staff: a long stick

"Sir," he said, "it is I who have called you together, but not because I have news of the return of my father, the renowned Odysseus. No. I would speak to you all because, for three years now, my mother has been troubled by men who come to demand that she choose one to marry. Day after day I see the fattest of my flocks and herds slaughtered, and the red wine poured out wastefully by these men who have come to woo my mother. They waste our goods and our wealth. If

I had reached manhood, I would defend my house against them. But as yet I am not able to do it, and so I have to stand by and see our house disgraced and ruined. Listen to your own consciences, and fear the anger of the gods. Do not allow this wrong to continue."

So Telemachus spoke. Then one of the suitors, Antinous, rose up. "Telemachus," said he, "why do you try to shame us in this way? We are not to blame, but your mother. Knowing that her husband Odysseus is dead, we have asked her to become the wife of one of us. But she gives us no honest answer. Instead she keeps us waiting by playing a trick on us."

Antinous went on: "I will tell all of you here how she tricked us. The lady Penelope set up a great loom and began to weave a wide web of cloth, to be used, she said, as a **shroud** for old Laertes, the father of Odysseus, when his time comes to die. She said that when she finished, she would choose a husband from among us. Months have gone by, and still it is not woven. But now we have heard from one of her handmaidens

shroud: a cloth used to wrap a dead person for burial

that what Penelope weaves in the daytime, she **unravels** at night. With this trick she tries to cheat us. So we will go on eating and drinking at her house, and giving orders to her servants. And we shall see which will satisfy her best—to give us an answer or to let the wealth of her house be wasted."

> **unravels:** takes apart the threads of

Then Antinous turned directly to Telemachus. "For you," he said, "I have these words. Take your mother to the house of her father, and have him give her in marriage to the one she chooses from among us. Do this and no more goods will be wasted."

Then Telemachus rose and said, "Never will I send my mother from the house my father brought her into. But you must leave my father's house, or the day may soon come when bad things will fall upon you for your disrespectful behavior."

Just then, Halitherses, a white-bearded old man who was skilled in interpreting signs, cried, "Behold!" And looking up they saw two eagles flying at full speed towards the place of assembly. The two great birds wheeled above and attacked each other fiercely with beak and claw, and then flew away across the city.

Then Halitherses spoke and told the meaning of the combat of the eagles in the air: "Listen, men of Ithaca. Odysseus is not far from his friends. For the suitors of Penelope, woe is coming. Therefore, I say to these men, put an end to your **mischief**."

> **mischief:** misbehavior, troublemaking

But the suitors only laughed at the old man. And one spoke out and said, "Even if Odysseus should return, that would not scare us. He is one, and we are many."

After this, the meeting broke up, and the suitors returned to the house of Odysseus.

Telemachus Prepares for a Voyage

Telemachus went to the shore of the sea, troubled by doubts about the voyage that Athena had commanded him to make. He dipped his hands into the water and prayed to the goddess for help.

Then he saw coming toward him an old man, Mentor, a friend of Odysseus famed for his wisdom. But by the grey, clear, shining eyes,

Telemachus knew that the figure was none other than the goddess Athena.

"Telemachus," said she, "I have seen in you something of the wisdom and the courage of Odysseus. If you are made of the same stuff as your father, then you will be neither fool nor coward. Listen, then, and do as I tell you. Go back to your father's house and get together barley flour and wine in jars. And while you are doing this I will gather a crew for your ship. I will find the best ship in Ithaca and we will **rig** her quickly and launch her on the wide deep."

rig: to make a sailboat ready to sail

Telemachus lost no time in doing as the goddess told him. He went back to the house and down into a **storeroom** filled with his father's treasures of gold and bronze, chests of clothing, and **casks** of wine. The strong doors of the room were kept closed, and night and day they were watched closely by Eurycleia, the faithful old housekeeper and childhood nurse.

storeroom: a room in which items are kept till needed

casks: large containers, such as barrels

Telemachus called Eurycleia to the storeroom and commanded her, "My nurse, fill twelve jars with wine for me now, and fill twelve leather bags with measures of **barley meal**. Get these things together at once, and say nothing about it—no one but yourself must know what I am doing. I will take everything away this evening as soon as my mother has gone upstairs for the night. I am going to Sparta and to Pylos to see if I can find out anything about the return of my father."

barley meal: a type of flour

When Eurycleia heard this she began to cry. "My dear child," she said, "whatever put such an idea into your head? Why in the world do you want to go—you, who are the one hope of the house? Your poor father is dead in some strange land, nobody knows where, and as soon as your back is turned these wicked ones here will be scheming to get rid of you. Oh, do not go wandering on the wide ocean."

"Dear nurse," answered Telemachus, "do not worry. I have been told to go by a goddess. Now make all ready for me as I have asked you, and swear to me that you will say nothing of it to my mother until twelve days have passed, unless she hears I have gone and asks you about it."

The old woman promised she would say nothing. Then she began drawing off the wine into jars, and getting the barley meal into the bags, while Telemachus went back to the suitors and listened to the minstrel sing about Odysseus and the wars of Troy.

While these things were happening, the goddess Athena went through the town in the shape of Telemachus. She asked a man named Noemon for the use of one of his swift ships, and he readily agreed. She enlisted many strong youths for the crew, and told them to meet at the ship by sundown.

When the ship was ready she went to the house of Odysseus and caused a deep sleep to fall upon the suitors. They laid their heads upon the tables and **slumbered** beside the wine cups. Then Athena again took the form and voice of old Mentor and called Telemachus to come outside.

slumbered: slept

"Come," she said, "the men are on board and at their oars, waiting for you to give your orders, so make haste and let us be off."

She led the way and Telemachus followed.

When they got to the ship they found the crew eagerly waiting. Telemachus climbed aboard, and Athena, in the likeness of old Mentor, took her place at the **helm**.

helm: the wheel for steering the ship

A wind filled the sails, and the youths pulled at the oars, and the ship dashed away. All night long Telemachus and his friends felt the ship bearing them swiftly onward through the dark water.

Telemachus Visits Nestor at Pylos

As the sun rose, Telemachus and his fellow voyagers drew near to the shore of Pylos. They saw great crowds on the shore engaged in ceremonies to honor Poseidon, the dark-haired god of the sea.

The voyagers brought their ship to the shore and Telemachus sprang from it. With him went the goddess, grey-eyed Athena, in the likeness of old Mentor. To Telemachus she said, "Go forward with a good heart, and ask Nestor, the king whom you have come to seek, for news of your father, Odysseus."

"But," said Telemachus, "how am I to speak to him? I am not used to holding long conversations

Selections from the Odyssey

Peisistratus brings Telemachus and Athena (disguised as Mentor) to King Nestor.

with people, and am hesitant to question one who is so much older than myself."

Athena encouraged him—the right words, she assured him, would come. She went quickly on, and Telemachus followed.

They found Nestor sitting with his sons, while around them people were busy preparing the feast. When they saw the strangers they rose to greet them. Nestor's son Peisistratus took the hand of Telemachus and the hand of the goddess and led them both to where Nestor was. Then he poured wine for them into a golden cup, and handed it to Athena first.

"Offer a prayer, sir, to Poseidon," said he, "for it is his feast that you are joining. Then pass the cup to your friend that he may do so also."

The goddess Athena, in the likeness of old Mentor, held the cup in her hand and offered a prayer to Poseidon. After Telemachus offered a prayer in similar words, the sons of Nestor urged them both to sit on some soft sheepskins spread on the shore. Dishes of meat were brought to them, and cups of wine, and when they had eaten, old King Nestor spoke.

"Until they have enjoyed food and drink," said the king, "it is not courteous to ask strangers who they are or where they are going. But now, my guests, I will ask what land you come from, what your **quest** may be, and what names you bear."

> **quest:** a search for something

Telemachus, encouraged by the king's kind manner, answered confidently: "Nestor, renowned king, glory of the Greeks, we have come out of Ithaca and we seek news of my father, Odysseus, who long ago fought by your side in the war of Troy. With you, men say, he sacked the great city of the Trojans. But we have heard nothing more of him. If you have any news to tell—whether you saw his death or have heard of his fate from another—I beg that you tell me all. And do not soften the tale out of kindness or pity. I pray you speak in truth to me, his son."

Then said old Nestor, "Truly, what **woeful** memories your words have awakened! Such long years of siege and battle, sleepless nights and challenging days. Oh, **ill-fated** land of Troy! There lies heroic Achilles, and also Patroclus—

> **woeful:** extremely sad
>
> **ill-fated:** unlucky; destined to have bad things happen

and there lies my own dear son, Antilochus, who was so swift and strong."

Nestor looked closely at Telemachus and continued: "And are you indeed the son of Odysseus? But why do I ask? When you speak, I seem to hear the very tones of his voice. He was my dear friend. But when the war was over, disasters came thick and fast. I myself, however, did not witness the good or evil fortunes of the other Greeks on their voyages home, and know only by **rumor** how they **fared**. But I would have you tell me of your homeland and of how things are in Ithaca."

rumor: uncertain reports; doubtful stories
fared: turned out

Telemachus agreed and told the old king of the evil deeds done by the suitors seeking to marry his mother. As he ended his tale, Telemachus cried out, "Oh, that the gods would give me such strength that I might take vengeance on these wicked men!"

Then Nestor spoke: "If Athena were to befriend you as she did your father, when we were fighting at Troy, he may yet return and punish these suitors. I never yet saw the gods so openly favor a man as Athena did Odysseus!"

Telemachus answered, "Even though the gods themselves may will it, I dare not let myself think of such good fortune."

Athena, in the likeness of Mentor, replied, "Telemachus, what are you talking about? If it should please them, any one of the gods could bring a man home from afar. Still, death is certain, and when a man's hour is come, not even the gods can save him, no matter how fond they are of him."

Then King Nestor spoke again to Telemachus. "Go to Menelaus in Sparta," he said. "It may be that he has news of Odysseus. You can go to Sparta in your ship, or if you wish to go by land, then will I give you a chariot and horses, and my son will go with you to guide you into Sparta."

With that, Telemachus and Athena rose to go back to their ship. But Nestor was not finished. He said, "Come with me to a place where you can rest comfortably. Let it never be said that a son of my dear friend Odysseus lay on the hard deck of a ship while there is room for guests in my hall. Come with me now."

Athena, in the likeness of old Mentor, said to

Nestor, "You have spoken well, renowned king. Telemachus should listen to you and go with you. But I shall return to the ship and stay with the young crew, for I am the only man of experience among them."

Suddenly the speaker vanished, and in his place a great eagle rose into the air and sped westwards towards the setting sun. All were speechless and amazed, until Nestor took Telemachus by the hand and broke the silence. "My friend," said he, "I see that you are going to be a great hero someday, since the gods favor you while you are still so young. This was none other than Zeus's mighty daughter, Athena, who honored your father so highly among the Greeks."

Telemachus went with Nestor and his sons to the high **citadel**, where he was given a bath and new clothes to wear. And in the morning, old king Nestor gave orders to prepare the chariot to take Telemachus to Sparta.

> **citadel:** a fortress that defends a city

Telemachus went into the chariot with Nestor's son Peisistratus. As the chariot sprang forward, they left behind the land of Pylos and made their way across the plain on the long journey to Sparta.

Telemachus in Sparta

Telemachus and Peisistratus came to Sparta, a country lying low among the hills. They brought the chariot to a halt outside the gate of the palace of King Menelaus. Upon this day, in preparation for the upcoming marriages of two of the king's children, there was feasting in the palace, and many relatives and neighbors were gathered there. Noticing the arrival of the visitors, a **steward** went to the king in his high hall.

steward: manager of a large household

"Renowned Menelaus," said the steward, "there are two strangers outside, men with the looks of heroes. Shall I invite them to enter, or shall I let them travel on to another **dwelling**?"

dwelling: a place where people live

"Why do you ask such a question?" said Menelaus in anger. "Have we not eaten the bread of other men on our wanderings, and have we not rested ourselves in other men's houses? Go now and invite them to enter and feast with us."

The steward hurried to lead Telemachus and Peisistratus into the palace. First they were invited to bathe, and when they had done so they were given new **cloaks** and shirts. Then they were led into the king's high hall. A clean table was set for them, and they were brought bread and meat, and also wine in cups of gold.

cloak: sleeveless coats that hang from the shoulders

Menelaus came to Telemachus and Peisistratus and said, "Welcome. Eat now, and when you have refreshed yourselves I will ask who you are and from what place you come."

When they had had enough to eat and drink, Telemachus whispered to the son of Nestor, "Look around, Peisistratus—see the gleam of bronze and gold, of amber, ivory, and silver. Everything in this house is so splendid that it is like seeing the palace of Zeus on high Olympus."

Menelaus overheard him and said, "My friend, no one can match the everlasting glories of immortal Zeus. And now, though I **dwell** in the midst of plenty, my heart is sad when I think of all those who perished on the plain of Troy. I often grieve for

dwell: live in a certain place

them, though for one man most of all. Of all the Greeks, none worked so hard or risked so much as he did. He was a man of many woes, and sorrowful is the **lot** of his wife Penelope and Telemachus his son."

lot: a person's situation or condition in life, especially as determined by fate

At this mention of his father, Telemachus could not control his tears. He covered his face with his cloak and wept.

Just then the lady Helen came into the high hall—Helen, for whom the kings and princes of Greece had gone to war. She gazed at Telemachus, and then, turning to her husband, she said, "Menelaus, never have I seen one so like Odysseus as this fair youth. Surely this is Telemachus, whom Odysseus left as a child, when, for my sake, the Greeks began their war against Troy."

"I see the likeness just as you do," Menelaus replied. "And when I made mention of Odysseus, he covered his face and wept. But can it indeed be that Telemachus has come into my house?"

"Renowned Menelaus," said Peisistratus, "this is indeed the son of Odysseus. And I am the son of another comrade of yours, of Nestor, who was with you at the war of Troy. I have been sent with Telemachus to guide him to your house."

Menelaus rose and said to Telemachus, "Never did there come to my house a youth more welcome. For my sake did Odysseus endure many hardships. But Odysseus, I know, has not returned to his own land of Ithaca."

Then Telemachus, thinking his father dead, or wandering lost through the world, wept. Helen, too, shed tears, remembering what had happened. And Menelaus, thinking upon Odysseus and on all his troubles, was silent and sad. And sad and silent too was Peisistratus, thinking upon Antilochus, his brother, who had perished in the war of Troy.

For many days Telemachus stayed in the house of King Menelaus, and Menelaus spoke to him of what happened at Troy and of the famous deeds of his father, Odysseus.

"After we had sacked King Priam's city, great suffering came upon us," said Menelaus. "Some of us sailed away, and some of us remained with King Agamemnon to make sacrifice to the gods. Then we parted on our separate ways, and death came to many. After many troubles, Agamemnon, my own brother, returned to his own land, but it would have been happier for him if he had died on the plain of Troy, for he was slain in his own house."

Menelaus went on: "And of your father, Telemachus, I can only tell you what was told to me on my homeward journey by **Proteus**, the ancient one of the sea, who sees past, present, and future. From him we learned that Odysseus was on a faraway island, with no ship and no companions, held there against his will by the **nymph** Calypso—and perhaps he may be there still. Odysseus was ever ready with a plan, and also greatly favored by the goddess Athena. For these reasons, Telemachus, be hopeful that your father will yet reach his own home and country."

> **The Shape-Shifter**
> In Greek mythology, Proteus was a shape-shifting god of the sea, with the power of prophecy. His name gives us the word *protean*, which means "constantly changing."

> **nymph:** in mythology, a nature spirit in the form of a beautiful young girl

Later in the night, as his comrade Peisistratus slept, Telemachus lay awake thinking about his father. And the goddess Athena came to him and said, "Telemachus, the time has come for you to return home. Go to Menelaus, and let him send you on your way."

When it was light, Telemachus went to Menelaus and told the king of his wish to return at once to his own country. "Telemachus," said Menelaus, "I will not keep you here. But first let me gather gifts for you."

With his wife Helen, Menelaus went down into his treasure-chamber and brought forth gifts. They came to Telemachus where he stood with Peisistratus by the chariot, waiting to depart. And Menelaus gave him a beautiful two-handled cup and a great bowl of silver, and Helen gave him an **embroidered** robe.

> **embroidered:** decorated with patterns or images sewn on with thread

"Dear child," she said, "take this robe. It is for your bride to wear upon her wedding day. Till then, have your dear mother keep it for you."

Then Menelaus poured wine out of a golden cup as an offering to the gods, and as he did, a bird flew over the horses' heads. It was an eagle, and it bore in its claws a goose from the farmyard.

"Hear me now," said Helen, "while I say what the gods have put in my heart. Just as this eagle came down from the hill and killed a goose of the farmyard, so will Odysseus come to his home and kill the suitors."

"May Zeus grant that it be so," said Telemachus.

As all things were now ready for his return to Ithaca, Telemachus touched the horses with his whip and they sped across the plain, for he was eager to return and keep an eye on the doings of the suitors.

A Mother Fears for Her Son

Meanwhile, in Ithaca the suitors were behaving as they had before. The two **ringleaders**, Antinous and Eurymachus, were sitting together when they were approached by Noemon, who had provided the ship for Telemachus.

> **ringleaders:** leaders of a group doing improper or illegal things

"Antinous," said Noemon, "do you know when Telemachus will return from Pylos? He has a ship of mine, and soon I will need it to transport some horses."

They were surprised when they heard this, for they thought that Telemachus was on a nearby farm, as he often was. Antinous asked, "When did he go? And what men did he take with him? Tell me truly, did you let him have the ship because he asked you, or did he take it without your permission?"

"He asked, and I loaned him the ship," answered Noemon. "I could not possibly refuse a man of his position. As for those who went with him, they were the best young men we have. I saw Mentor go on board as captain — or it may have been some god in his likeness, for I saw Mentor yesterday in the city, and no ship has arrived at Ithaca since they sailed."

As Noemon left, Antinous said to the other suitors, "Telemachus has got away. Now hear me. Let us prepare a ship with a crew of twenty men, and wait for him in the narrow sea he must pass through as he nears Ithaca. There, we will cut short his adventures. He will regret the day that he set out to try and get news of his father!"

The suitors cheered their approval and left to put the plan into action. They did not know that, hiding behind a fence, a servant named Medon had overheard what Antinous said. Without delay

Medon went in search of Penelope, who was still unaware of her son's departure. He found her sitting with her handmaidens in her **chamber**.

chamber: room, especially a bedroom

As Medon stood in the doorway to Penelope's room, she looked up and said, "Medon, have the suitors sent you here? Do they demand that my handmaidens leave their tasks and cook dinner for them? May this be the last **morsel** they ever taste!"

morsel: small bit of food

Medon said, "My lady, it is something much worse. Telemachus has sailed to Pylos to get news of his father, and the suitors are plotting to slay him on his way home."

Medon left Penelope in great grief, surrounded by her weeping handmaidens. "First I lost my brave husband," said Penelope. "And now my son is at the mercy of the winds and waves. And I never heard one word about his leaving home."

Then turning to her handmaidens she cried, "Hearts of stone, why did you not tell me of his going? If I had known, I might have stopped him."

Then the old nurse Eurycleia, who was sitting among the women, said, "You may kill me, or let me live on in your house, whichever you please, but I will tell you the truth. I knew all about it, and gave Telemachus barley meal and wine for his journey. But he made me swear a solemn oath that I would not tell you anything for some twelve days, unless you asked or happened to hear of his leaving, for he did not want the tears to flow down your fair cheeks. But now, dear lady, wash your face, change your dress, and go upstairs with your maids to pray to Athena, and ask her to keep your son from harm."

Penelope was comforted and dried her tears. She went with her handmaidens to the upper chamber, where she knelt before the shrine of Athena and prayed for the safety of her son. Then she sank down on a couch, exhausted by her emotions.

ATHENA APPEARS IN THE GUISE OF PENELOPE'S SISTER.

Athena heard her prayer, and to **soothe** Penelope's troubled spirit the goddess made a vision in the shape and appearance of a beloved sister of the queen.

soothe: to calm, to bring relief to

And the vision slipped through the doorway and came to Penelope's bedside and said, "Take heart. Your son will come back to you, He has a mighty helper by his side, Athena herself, who sent me here to strengthen and comfort you." Then the vision vanished, and Penelope rose refreshed and comforted.

Meanwhile, Antinous had taken steps to carry out his wicked plan. At nightfall he went down to the sea with twenty men and boarded a ship. They sailed out to the middle of the **strait** between Ithaca and a small neighboring island. There they anchored, and waited for the coming of Telemachus.

strait: a narrow passage of water connecting two larger bodies of water

Odysseus and Calypso

In high Olympus, the gods met in council, and Athena reminded them of the many sufferings of Odysseus.

"Father Zeus," she said, "I fear that Odysseus is forgotten, even by his subjects, whom he ruled as a kind father. For years, he has been suffering on an island, held against his will by the nymph Calypso. She will not let him go. She keeps trying to make him forget his home, while he, poor man, thinks of nothing else. But he cannot get back to his own country, for he can find neither ships nor sailors to take him over the sea. And now wicked people are trying to murder his only son, Telemachus, who is coming home from Pylos and Sparta, where he has traveled to see if he can get news of his father."

"My child," replied Zeus, "you know well that you are perfectly able to protect Telemachus and see him safely home again."

Then Zeus spoke to Hermes: "Hermes, be our messenger in this, and go and tell Calypso we have **decreed** that Odysseus is to return home."

decreed: ordered; proclaimed as an official order

Thus spoke Zeus, and without delay Hermes bound his glittering golden sandals with which he could fly like the wind over land and sea. He swooped down through the clouds till he reached the level of the sea, flying till he came to the island and the cave where the nymph Calypso lived.

Across the cave grew a **straggling** vine, heavy with clusters of grapes. Calypso was within the cave, and as Hermes came near, he heard her singing one of her magic songs and saw her weaving at her loom.

> **straggling:** spreading in an irregular way

Calypso recognized Hermes at once. "Hermes," she said, "honored and ever welcome, why have you come to see me? Say what you want, and I will do it for you at once if I can. But let me set refreshment before you."

She drew a table loaded with **ambrosia** beside him and mixed him some red **nectar**. Hermes ate and drank, and then said, "You ask me why I have come here. Zeus sent me. He says that you hold here the most ill-fated of all those who fought nine years before the city of King Priam and sailed home in the tenth year after sacking the city. Zeus says that you are to let this man go at once, for it is decreed that he shall not perish here, far from his own people, but

> **ambrosia:** in Greek mythology, the food of the gods
>
> **nectar:** in Greek mythology, the drink of the gods

shall return to his house and country and see his friends again."

"Oh," cried Calypso, "woe to any immortal who loves a mortal, for the gods are always jealous of their love. I do not hold Odysseus here because I hate him, but because I love him greatly and would have him dwell with me here. And I would make him an immortal so that he would know neither old age nor death."

"He does not desire to be freed from old age and death," said Hermes. "He desires to return to his own land and to live with his dear wife, Penelope, and his son, Telemachus. And Zeus, the greatest of the gods, commands that you let him go upon his way."

"I have no ship to give him," said Calypso, "and no company of men to help him to cross the sea."

"He must leave the island and cross the sea — Zeus commands it," Hermes said.

"If it must be so, then I must help him make his way," Calypso said. Then she bowed her head and Hermes left her.

Calypso went down to the shore. There stood

Odysseus, looking across the wide sea with tears in his eyes.

She said to him, "Odysseus, leave your sorrow. The time has come for you to depart from my island. Go and cut some beams of wood, and make yourself a large raft to carry you over the sea. I will put bread, wine, and water on board to save you from starving. I will also give you clothes and send you a fair wind to take you home, if the gods above will it—for they know more about these things than I."

"Now goddess," answered Odysseus, "there is something behind all this. You cannot really mean to help me when you tell me to put to sea on a raft. How shall a man cross this vast sea on a raft? Solemnly swear that you intend me no harm."

Calypso smiled. "May heaven and earth be my witnesses that I mean you no harm. Come now, and I will help you on your way."

She brought him to the side of the island where great trees grew, and she put in his hands a double-edged axe. Then Odysseus felled twenty trees with his axe of bronze. Day after day he worked to build the raft. He set a mast upon it and fixed a **rudder** to guide it. Calypso wove him a web of cloth for sails.

On the fifth day Calypso gave him garments for the journey and brought **provisions** down to the raft. She showed Odysseus how to guide his course by the star that some call the Bear.

> **rudder:** a flat piece that sits in the water and can be moved to steer a boat
>
> **provisions:** supplies such as food and water

"Good luck go with you," she said to Odysseus. "But if you could only know how much suffering is in store for you before you get back to your own country, you would stay where you are, and let me make you immortal, no matter how anxious you may be to see your wife, whom you think of all the time, day after day. Is your Penelope so rare that you prefer her to me? How is it that a mortal woman should compare in beauty with an immortal?"

"Goddess," replied Odysseus, "do not be angry with me. I know you are far lovelier than my wife Penelope, for you are an immortal goddess, and she is but a mortal woman. Nevertheless I long day and night to see her face. I want to get home, and can think of nothing else. If some god wrecks me on the dark sea, I will bear it and make the best of it. Long have I toiled, and much have I suffered, on land and sea. If more remains, I will endure that also."

So saying, Odysseus took his place on the raft and sailed away from the island where Calypso had held him for so long. But the winds blew upon his raft and the waves dashed against it. A fierce gust broke the mast in the middle, and the sail sank into the deep. Then Odysseus was flung down on the raft. For a long time he lay there, overwhelmed by the water that broke over him, as the winds drove the raft **to and fro**.

> **to and fro:** constantly moving from side to side

In the depths of the sea there was a nymph who saw his troubles and who had pity upon him. Ino was her name. She rose from the waves in the likeness of a seagull, and she sat upon the raft and spoke to Odysseus.

"Unfortunate man," she said, "Poseidon, the god of the sea, is still angry with you, and the waters may destroy the raft to which you cling. Then there would be no hope for you. But do what I say and you shall escape. Take this veil from me and wind it around your chest. As long as it is upon you, you cannot drown. But when you reach the mainland, untie the veil and **cast** it into the sea so that it may come back to me."

cast: throw

She gave him the veil and then dived into the sea and the waves closed over her. Odysseus took the veil and wound it around his chest. Then a great wave came and shattered the raft. He grabbed onto a single piece of wood, and, with the veil bound across his chest, for two nights and two days he was tossed about on the waters. On the third day, when dawn came the winds calmed, and he saw land very near. He swam eagerly towards it. But when he drew nearer he heard the crash of waves as they struck against the rocks.

A great wave flung him towards the shore. His bones would have been broken upon the rocks if he had not been ready-minded enough to rush towards a rock and cling to it with both hands until the wave dashed by. But the retreating waves carried him back to the deep with the skin stripped from his hands. The waves closed over him. When he rose again he swam round looking for a place where there might be no rocks but instead some opening into the land.

At last he saw the mouth of a river. With his

flesh swollen and streams of salt water gushing from his mouth and nostrils, he swam. At last he reached land. He lay gasping on the ground, fainting with terrible weariness.

In a while his breath came back and his courage rose. He remembered the veil that the sea-nymph had given him and he loosened it and let it fall back into the flowing river. A wave came and carried it back to Ino, who caught it in her hands.

Odysseus climbed from the cold of the river up to the woods, where he found two olive trees growing side by side, making a shelter against the winds. He lay between them, covered himself with leaves, and slept.

Odysseus and Nausicaa

The land on which Odysseus had been cast like a piece of broken wreckage was called Phaeacia. Its people were famous **mariners** who had grown rich through trade.

mariners: sailors

As Odysseus slept, the goddess Athena went to the city of the Phaeacians. She came to the palace of Alcinous, king of the Phaeacians, and passed through all the doors till she came to where the king's daughter, Nausicaa, slept. She entered into Nausicaa's dream, appearing to her as one of her girl-comrades. And in the dream she spoke to the princess.

"Nausicaa," she said, "here are your clothes all lying in disorder—and yet your marriage day will be soon—a day when you must have clean clothing for yourself and for your bridesmaids. There is much to be done, Nausicaa. Be ready at daybreak, and take your maidens with you, and bring the garments of your household to the river to be washed. I will come and help you. Ask your father to give you a wagon and mules to carry all the garments to the riverside."

When Nausicaa rose, she remembered her dream and went through the palace and found her father just as he was about join a meeting of the assembly of the Phaeacians.

"Father dear," she said, "would you let me use a big wagon? I want to take all our dirty clothes to the river and wash them. You should have a clean shirt when you attend meetings of the council, and my brothers like to have clean linen when they go to dances."

She did not say a word about her own wedding, for she was a little shy, but her father understood and replied, "You shall have whatever you need. The men shall get you a good strong wagon that will hold all the clothes."

He ordered his men to get the wagon and mules ready. Then Nausicaa gathered her handmaidens together and they brought the soiled garments of the household to the wagon. Her mother added a basket filled with good things to eat and a skin of wine, so that Nausicaa and her maids might not go hungry while they were away. She gave them a jar of olive oil, too, so that they might rub themselves with oil when bathing in the river.

Young Nausicaa herself drove the wagon to the riverbank. The girls brought the garments to the stream, and in the shallow parts **trod** them with their bare feet. When they finished washing the garments, they left them on the clean pebbles to dry in the sun. Then Nausicaa and her companions went into the river and bathed in the water.

Afterward, they sat down and ate their meal.

trod: stepped on

Then, as the garments were not yet dried, Nausicaa called on her companions to play. They took a ball and threw it from one to the other, singing a song that went with the game.

The princess threw the ball, and the girl whose turn it was to catch missed it. The ball went into the river and was carried down the stream. At that they all raised a cry—a cry that woke **Odysseus** who was sleeping, covered with leaves, in the shelter of the two olive trees.

He crept out, looking like a hungry lion battered by rain and wind who goes forth in a storm to seek his **prey**. When he saw the girls in the meadow he wanted to go to them to beg for help. But when they looked on him they were frightened and they ran and hid themselves. Only Nausicaa stood still, for Athena put courage into her heart.

prey: an animal hunted by another for food

Odysseus stood a little way from her and spoke. "Have pity on me!" he began. "Are you a goddess or a mortal woman? If you are a goddess, you seem to me most like to **Artemis**, daughter of great Zeus. But if you are mortal, then

Artemis: in Greek mythology, the goddess of the hunt, of wild animals, and of the moon

your father and mother are blessed indeed. And happy above all will he be who will lead you to his home as his bride."

And still Nausicaa stood, and Odysseus was filled with respect for her, so noble she seemed. "O lady," he said, "have pity on me, for you are the first person I have met, and I know no one else in this country. I am a man of many woes. Yesterday I was flung on this coast, after a voyage of twenty days. Give me an old garment to wear and show me the way to the town. And may the gods grant you all your heart's desire."

To this Nausicaa answered, "You shall not want for clothes nor for anything else that a stranger **in distress** may need. I will show you the way to the town, as well."

in distress: in trouble, in great need

Odysseus asked what land he was in. "This," Nausicaa replied, "is the land of the Phaeacians, and Alcinous is king over them. And I am the king's daughter, Nausicaa."

Then she called to her companions. "Do not hide," she said. "This is no enemy, but some poor man who has lost his way. We must be kind to him, for strangers in distress are under Zeus's protection. So, girls, give the poor fellow something to eat and drink, and let him wash in the stream at some place sheltered from the wind."

The girls came back and brought Odysseus to a sheltered place, and they laid a garment beside him. One brought the jar of olive oil to use when he bathed in the river. And Odysseus was very glad to get this oil, for his back and shoulders were all crusted over with salt from the sea.

He went into the river and bathed and rubbed himself with the oil. Then he put on the garment that had been given him. So well he looked that when he came towards them again the princess Nausicaa said to her handmaidens, "Look now on the man who seemed so terrifying! He is most noble in appearance. Now, my maidens, bring the stranger meat and drink."

They came and set food before Odysseus, who ate and drank hungrily, for it was long since he had had food of any kind. And while he ate, Nausicaa and her companions gathered the garments that were now dried, singing songs the while. They folded the garments and put them on the wagon.

When they were ready to go, Nausicaa said to Odysseus, "Stranger, if you wish to go to the city, come with us now so that we may guide you. As we go through the fields and by the farms, walk behind and keep near the wagon. But when we enter the city, go no further with us. People might speak unkindly of me if they saw me with a stranger such as you. They might say, 'Who does Nausicaa bring to her father's house? Some **seafaring** man she would like to make her husband, most likely.' To prevent such rude gossip, I would have you come on your own to my father's house."

seafaring: regularly traveling by sea

Nausicaa continued, "When you come into the city, ask the way to the house of my father, Alcinous. Any child can point it out to you, for no one has so fine a house. When you have entered the gates, go right across the inner courtyard till you come to where my mother sits weaving yarn by the light of the fire. My father will be sitting near, drinking his wine in the evening. Pass by his seat and come to my mother, and bow down at her knees and ask for her aid. If you win her over, then you will be helped by our people and be given the means of returning to your own land."

ODYSSEUS FOLLOWS NAUSICAA AND HER COMPANIONS.

Then Nausicaa called to the mules and the wagon moved on, with Odysseus following behind. As the sun was setting and they neared the city, they came to a **grove** dedicated to the goddess Athena. As Nausicaa and her maidens went on, Odysseus waited in the grove, and he prayed to the goddess: "Hear me, Athena, and grant that I may come before the king of this land as one well worthy of his aid."

grove: a group of trees

Odysseus and the Phaeacians

About the time that Nausicaa arrived at her father's house, Odysseus left the grove of Athena and went into the city. He soon came to the palace of King Alcinous, with its doors of gold and silver and bronze.

He went through the courtyard to a great hall. On that evening, the leading men of the Phaeacians sat with the king. Odysseus passed by them and, as Nausicaa had advised, went directly to where Arete, the queen, sat. And he knelt before her and spoke humbly.

"O Queen Arete!" Odysseus began. "May the gods give all who are here a happy life. I have come to beg that you put me on my way to my own land, for long have I suffered far from my home and friends."

Then he sat down by the **hearth** in the ashes near the fire, and for a while not a word was spoken, but all sat gazing at him in wonder.

> **hearth:** area in front of a fireplace

Then one of the nobles in the hall—the oldest man then living in that land—said, "King

Alcinous, do not let this stranger sit there among the ashes. Tell him to sit upon a chair, and give him something to eat and drink."

Alcinous took Odysseus by the hand and raised him from where he sat, and asked his son to rise and let the stranger sit in his place. Odysseus sat on a chair inlaid with silver, and the housemaid brought him wine and good things to eat.

King Alcinous turned to the gathered people and announced, "This man begs that we take him to his home. Tomorrow we will have an assembly, and will consider how we may best do this."

All agreed, and then rose to go back to their own houses. Odysseus was left alone in the hall with the king and the queen. Looking closely at Odysseus, the queen recognized the mantle he wore, for she herself had made it with her handmaidens. She said to Odysseus, "Stranger, from what country have you come, and who gave you these clothes?"

Then Odysseus told her how he had traveled many miles across the sea on the raft, and how the raft had been broken, and how he had at last reached the shore, and how Nausicaa had found him. Said Odysseus, "After I lay among the leaves all night long, then down to the river came your daughter. I heard her playing with her friends, and to her I made my plea for help. She gave me these garments, and she showed an understanding that was far beyond her years."

Then Alcinous said, "Our daughter did not do well when she did not bring you straight to our house."

Odysseus said, "My lord, do not blame her. She told me to follow with her handmaidens, and she was only careful that no one should have cause to make disrespectful remarks regarding the stranger whom she found. I thought you might be displeased if you saw me, so I came alone, as every human being is sometimes a little suspicious."

"Stranger," replied Alcinous, "I am not the kind of man to get angry about nothing. It is always better to be reasonable. And now that I see what kind of person you are, I wish you would stay here. But if it is not your will to stay, then I will give you a ship and a company of men to take you to your own land, no matter how far away it may be. We Phaeacians have no equals in seamanship, and no ships in all the world are like mine."

The next day, Alcinous addressed the crowd gathered for the assembly: "This stranger has come to my hall. I do not know who he is, or where he comes from, whether from the east or the west. And he begs us to transport him safely to his home. As we have done for others in times past, let us help him in his journey. And even now let us make a ship ready for the voyage, and put two and fifty of our noblest youths upon it. But before he departs from us, come to my hall and feast. And let the minstrel come also, blind Demodocus, whose songs will make us glad at the feast."

So the king led the men to the palace for the feast. And one was sent to bring the minstrel, blind Demodocus. To him the gods had given a good and an evil fortune—the gift of song with the lack of sight.

Demodocus was placed on a seat inlaid with silver, and he hung his **lyre** on the **pillar** by his seat. When the guests and the minstrel had feasted, blind Demodocus took down the lyre and sang of things that were already

lyre: a small U-shaped harp

pillar: a column; a tall post used for support in a building

BLIND DEMODOCUS SINGS OF THE DEEDS OF HEROES.

famous—of the deeds of Achilles and Odysseus.

When he heard the minstrel's words, Odysseus caught up his cloak and drew it over his face. Tears were falling down his cheeks and he was ashamed of being seen. No one noticed his weeping except Alcinous, and the king wondered why his guest should be so moved by the minstrel's song.

When they had feasted, Alcinous said, "Let us

go forth now and engage in games and sports so that our guest may one day tell his friends what our young men can do."

All went to the place where the games were played. There was a foot race, followed by matches of wrestling, boxing, leaping, and throwing weights. All the youths present took part in the games.

As the sports were ending, Laodamas, the son of King Alcinous, said to his friends, "Come, let us ask the stranger whether he is skilled in any sport." And he went to Odysseus and said, "Friend and stranger, come and join the games. Cast away your cares, for your journey shall not be long delayed. Even now the ship is prepared and we have with us the company of youths that will help you to your own land."

Odysseus said, "I am in no mind for sport and games. I can think only of getting back to my home."

Then a youth named Euryalus, who had won the wrestling match, said rudely, "Well, stranger, you do not look like a man skillful in boxing and wrestling, but like one who travels about to buy and sell."

Then Odysseus answered with a stern look, "Young man, you have fine looks but no grace in thought or speech. And you have stung me with your words. Broken as I am, I will give proof of my strength."

Without waiting to throw off his cloak, Odysseus sprang up and grabbed a heavy disc of iron, far heavier than those the Phaeacians had been throwing. With one whirl he flung it from his hands, far beyond the longest throw of the Phaeacian athletes.

Odysseus said, "Let any one match this throw, if he can. And if any of you would challenge me in boxing or wrestling or even in the foot race, let him stand forward—any except the sons of Alcinous, for it would not be right to compete against the family of my host."

Not one of the Phaeacians took up the challenge, but all sat gazing in awe at the stranger. Then King Alcinous said, "So that you may have something to tell your friends when you are in your own land, we shall show you the games in which we are most skillful. For we Phaeacians are not perfect boxers or wrestlers, but we excel in running and in dancing and in pulling with the oar." Then he called out, "You **nimble** dancers! Come forward and show your skill."

> **nimble:** quick and graceful in movement

A space was cleared for the dance, and the blind minstrel, Demodocus, played his lyre. Odysseus **marveled** at the dancers' grace and spirit. When the dance was ended he said to the king, "You said your people were nimble dancers, and indeed they have proved themselves to be so. I was filled with wonder as I watched them."

> **marveled:** felt great wonder and amazement

Alcinous spoke to his people and said, "This stranger, in all that he does and says, shows himself to be a wise and a mighty man. Let us now give him gifts, that he may remember us, and rejoice in spirit when he thinks of his stay in Phaeacia. Here there are twelve princes of the Phaeacians, and I make a thirteenth. Let each of us give him a worthy gift, and then let us go back to my house and sit down to supper. As for Euryalus, let him make amends to the stranger for his rudeness of speech as he offers him his gift."

All approved the king's words, and Euryalus

went to Odysseus and said, "Stranger, if I have said anything that offended you, may the winds blow it away, and may the gods grant you a safe return, for I understand you have been long away from home, and have gone through much hardship."

So saying, Euryalus gave Odysseus a sword of bronze with a silver **hilt** and a **sheath** of ivory. Odysseus took it and said, "Good luck to you too my friend, and may the gods grant you every happiness. I hope you will never miss the sword you have given me."

> **hilt:** the handle of a sword or dagger
>
> **sheath:** a case for the blade a sword or knife

Each of the twelve princes gave gifts to Odysseus, and the gifts were brought to the palace and left by the side of the queen. And Arete herself gave Odysseus a beautiful chest with fine clothing in it, and King Alcinous gave him a beautiful cup made of gold.

In the palace a bath was prepared for Odysseus, and he entered it and was glad, for not since he had left the island of Calypso had he enjoyed a warm bath. He came from the bath and put on the beautiful garment that had been given to him, and as he walked through the hall he looked like a king among men.

The maiden Nausicaa stood by a pillar as he passed. And she spoke to him and said, "Farewell, stranger! And when you are in your own country, think sometimes of me, Nausicaa, who helped you."

Odysseus took her hand and said, "Farewell, daughter of King Alcinous! May Zeus grant that I return to my own land, where every day I shall honor you in my memory, for to you I owe my life."

Then he went into the hall, where he was seated by the side of the king. The minstrel, blind Demodocus, was brought in. And when supper was served, Odysseus was given the tasty part of a wild boar that is served to a guest whom his host wishes to honor above all others. And Odysseus in turn sent to Demodocus the best portion of his own meat.

When all had had enough of meat and drink, Odysseus praised the minstrel, saying, "You sing so well of the Greeks at Troy, of all their sufferings and adventures, that it is as if you had been there yourself. Now I would ask if you can sing of the Wooden Horse that brought destruction to the Trojans."

Demodocus took down the lyre and sang. The minstrel sang how the Wooden Horse was made, and how Odysseus, with the bravest of the Greek chiefs, hid themselves within, and how the rest of the forces pretended to depart, sailing away in their ships, though they did not sail farther than to a nearby island. Also he sang of how the people of Troy talked of what should be done with so wonderful a thing—whether to break it open, or drag it into the sea, or respect it as an offering to the gods. And he sang of how the people pulled the horse within the walls of the city, and how Odysseus and his comrades poured forth from the hollow of the horse and took the city.

As the minstrel sang, the heart of Odysseus melted within him and tears fell down his cheeks. And when Alcinous saw him weeping, he cried out, "Let the minstrel cease, for there is one among us to whom his song is not pleasing—the stranger here, who has tears flowing down his cheeks."

The minstrel ceased, and all the company looked in surprise at Odysseus, who sat with his head bowed and his cloak wrapped around his head.

Then Alcinous spoke again. "Any right-thinking person," said the king, "knows that he ought to treat a guest as though he were his own brother—and you, unknown guest, are as a brother to us. But now, will you not be brotherly to us as well? Tell us by what name you are called in your own land. Tell us of your land and city. Tell us of your wanderings, and say why you weep over the tale of the Greeks at the war of Troy. Did you have a relative or dear friend who died on the plains of Troy?"

All the guests bent forward. Long had they wanted to know the stranger's identity. And now, their curiosity, which had been **held in check** by their customs of courtesy, was set free by the questions of King Alcinous.

> **held in check:** held back, kept down, kept under control

After a moment's pause, Odysseus turned to the gathered company and said, "King Alcinous, it is a good thing to hear a minstrel with such a sweet voice as Demodocus has. For me, there is nothing better than when the tables are loaded with bread and meats and cups of good wine, and people come together with open hearts, and a minstrel sings noble songs. This seems to me to be happiness indeed. But you have asked me to speak of my wanderings and my toils. Ah, where can I begin that tale? For the gods have given me more woes than a man can speak of!

"But first I will tell you my name and my country. I am Odysseus, son of Laertes, and my land is Ithaca, a rugged isle and the home of many brave men—and for me, at least, there is no place fairer than a man's own land."

And then Odysseus began to tell his tale, which kept his hearers **spellbound** until far into the night.

> **spellbound:** fascinated, captivated, completely in attention

Odysseus Begins His Story: The Cyclops

[Here Odysseus himself tells the story of his adventures after the fall of Troy.]

Now I will tell you the tale of my wanderings, and of all the troubles that the gods laid upon me as I journeyed from Troy.

The wind bore my ships from the coast of Troy, and swept us from our course. For nine days we were driven away from all known lands. On the tenth day we came to a strange country. The people of that land were harmless and friendly, but the land itself was most dangerous. For in that land grew the honey-sweet fruit of the lotus that makes people forgetful of their past and **neglectful** of their future.

> **neglectful:** not caring about, not paying attention to

The lotus-eaters offered my men the sweet fruit of the lotus to eat. And those of my men who ate it forgot their friends and their home, and had no desire in life but to remain there all their days and feast with the lotus-eaters. They wept as I forced them back to the ships, and I had to place them beneath the benches and tie their hands and feet. We took to the oars and left that place in haste.

Later we came to the land of the Cyclops, a giant people. Just outside the harbor of their land, there is an empty island with a well of bright water, where we **beached** our ships and took down our sails.

> **beached:** ran the ships onto the beach

We looked across to the land of the Cyclops,

and we heard the sound of voices and saw the smoke of fires and heard the bleating of flocks of sheep and goats. I called my companions together and said, "Stay here, most of you, as I go with my own ship and men to find out what kind of people live there, and whether they will treat us kindly and give us provisions for our voyage."

We soon came to their land and saw a cave near the sea. Round the cave there were flocks of sheep and goats. I took twelve men with me and I left the rest to guard the ship.

I had with me a goat-skin full of wine, dark red and sweet. So **potent** was this wine, and the smell of it so sweet, that no man could easily resist drinking it. I had this great skin of wine with me, for I felt in my heart that I would need it.

potent: powerful

We went into the cave and it seemed to be the dwelling of some rich and skillful shepherd. There were pens for the young of the sheep and goats, and there were baskets full of cheeses, and full milk-pails lined up along the wall. But we found no one there.

My men wanted me to take

kids: young goats

some of the cheeses and some of the lambs and **kids** and go back to our ship. But this I would not do, for I wanted to find out who this shepherd might be, and if he would be willing to help us strangers, as he should, by freely giving us things from his own supply of goods.

It was evening when the Cyclops came home. Never in our lives did we see a creature so frightful. He was a giant in size, and he had but one eye, and that eye was in his forehead.

He carried on his shoulder a great pile of wood for his fire, which he threw down with a great crash. We fled in terror into the dark, hidden parts of the cave. Next he drove his flocks into the cave and closed the entrance with a huge stone that not all our combined strength could move. Then he milked his **ewes** and goats, and half of the milk he used for cheese, and half he set aside for himself. He lit a fire with the pine logs, and when it blazed up he saw me and my comrades.

ewes: female sheep

"Who are you?" cried Polyphemus, for that was the giant's name. "Are you traders? Or do you sail the sea as pirates?"

Our hearts were shaken with terror at the sound of his deep voice. I answered him, saying, "We are not pirates, but Greeks sailing back from Troy. We are the people of the great King Agamemnon, whose fame is spread far and wide. And in the name of Zeus, who rewards or punishes hosts and guests, we humbly ask you to help us, as visitors may reasonably expect."

He answered me saying, "We Cyclops do not care about Zeus or any of your gods. I will give you nothing for the sake of Zeus, but only if I am in the mood to do so. But come, tell me, where have you left your ship?"

I knew it would be better not to let the Cyclops know where my ship and companions were. So I tricked him by saying that my ship had been broken on the rocks, and that I and the men with me were the only ones who had escaped alive.

Without saying a word, he grabbed two of my men and, swinging them by the legs, dashed their brains out on the earth. He tore them apart and, like a lion in the wilderness, devoured them, taking huge swallows of milk between mouthfuls, leaving not a morsel, not even the bones.

When we saw so terrible a sight, we could only weep and pray to Zeus for help. And when the giant had had his fill of human flesh and the milk of his flocks, he lay down among his sheep and went to sleep beside the fire.

Then I considered whether I should take my sharp sword in my hand and **pierce** the giant's heart. But second thoughts held me back. I might be able to kill him as he slept, but not even with my companions could I roll away the great stone that closed the mouth of the cave.

pierce: stab

Dawn came, and the Cyclops awakened, lit his fire, and milked his flocks. Then he clutched up two more of my men and began eating them for his morning's meal. After this, he rolled away the great stone and drove his flocks out of the cave, and he put the stone back over the mouth of the cave.

All that day I was thinking what I might do to save myself and my companions. In the cave, there was a huge pole, the green wood of an olive-tree, big as a ship's mast, which the Cyclops planned to use as a walking-staff. I and my companions cut off a **fathom's length** of the wood and

fathom's length: six feet

sharpened it to a point. We hardened it in the fire, and then hid it away.

At evening the giant came back and drove his sheep into the cave, and the **rams** as well, which he had left outside before. Then he closed the cave again with the stone and milked his ewes and his goats. And, as before, he took two of my comrades and devoured them.

rams: male sheep

When he had finished, I went to the terrible creature with a bowl of wine in my hands—the dark, sweet, potent wine that no man can resist. He drank it and cried out, "Give me another bowl of this, and tell me your name, so that I may give you a gift for bringing me this honey-tasting drink."

Then I filled the bowl again, and he drank. Three times I gave it to him, and three times he drank. And I spoke to him with **cunning** and said, "Noman is my name. Noman is what my father and mother and my friends have always called me. And now, give me your gift."

cunning: trickiness, craftiness

"Give me more of the drink, Noman," he shouted. "And my gift to you is this—you shall be eaten last." And as he said this, he fell back in a drunken sleep.

ODYSSEUS FILLS THE CYCLOPS' BOWL WITH POTENT WINE.

Then I, with my remaining companions, took up the beam of olive wood that we had made into a hard and pointed stake. We thrust it into the ashes of the fire. When the pointed end began to glow we drew it out of the flame. Then we grasped the great stake and, dashing at the Cyclops, thrust it into his eye.

The giant leapt up and tore away the stake and cried aloud—so loud that all the other Cyclops who dwelt on the mountainside heard him and rushed to his cave, asking him, "Polyphemus, why do you shout and wake us out of sleep? Is someone stealing your sheep or hurting you?"

And the giant bellowed, "Noman! Noman is hurting me!"

"Well," said the other Cyclops, "if no man is hurting you, then it must be the gods, and we cannot help you with that." And they went away from the mouth of the cave.

Then, groaning with pain, Polyphemus felt about with his hands till he found the stone, and he rolled it away from the mouth of the cave. He sat in the doorway and stretched out his hands to catch anyone going out with the sheep, for he thought we might be foolish enough to dash out.

I thought hard about how I could save myself and my companions. I thought and thought, for our lives depended on it. In the end I came up with this plan.

The giant had driven the rams along with the other sheep into the cave, and for this I thanked Zeus, because the rams were large and strong, with heavy black **fleece**. I fastened my comrades under the bellies of the beasts, tying them with willow twigs, of which

fleece: a sheep's wooly covering

the giant made his bed. I bound the rams together in threes—I tied a man beneath each middle ram, and then set one ram on either side. Thus every three rams carried a man.

There was one mighty ram far larger than all the others. I placed myself under him, clinging to the wool of his belly, grasping tight with both my hands. So we all waited, and when the morning came, the rams rushed forth to the pasture. As they passed through the doorway of the cave, Polyphemus felt the back of each, but he did not think to check underneath.

Last of all went the great ram, under which I was hidden. The Cyclops knew him as he passed, and placed his hands on him, and said, "What's this? You, the leader of the flock, are always the first to run to the pastures in the morning, but now you are last of all. Are you troubled for your poor master? Oh, how I wish you could tell me where this Noman has hidden himself."

He let the ram pass out of the cave. When we were out of reach of the giant, I let go of the ram and set my companions free. We gathered together many of Polyphemus's sheep and drove them down to our ship. Then we took to the oars and pulled away from the accursed land.

When we had rowed just far enough that a man's voice could still be heard from the shore, I stood up and shouted, "Cyclops, your evil deeds have been justly punished!"

Enraged, Polyphemus broke off the top of a great hill and hurled it where he had heard my voice. Right in front of the ship's **bow** it fell, and a great wave rose and washed the ship back to the shore. But with both hands I **seized** a long pole and pushed the ship from the land, and signaled my men to row with all their might.

> **bow:** the front end of a ship
>
> **seized:** forcefully grabbed

The men bent to the oars and pulled the ship away or it would have been broken by the great rocks that Polyphemus threw. And when we were farther away I shouted to him, "Cyclops, if any man should ask you who put out your eye, say that it was Odysseus of Ithaca, the son of Laertes."

Then I heard Polyphemus cry out, "I call upon Poseidon, the god of the sea, whose son I am, to avenge me upon Odysseus. Poseidon, grant that Odysseus may never reach his home alive. Or if he must get back to his friends at last, let him do so only after much toil and suffering, all his comrades lost, in great danger, and on a stranger's ship, to find sorrow in his home."

So Polyphemus prayed, and Poseidon heard his prayer. But we went on in our ship, rejoicing at our escape. We came to where my other ships were waiting. All the company rejoiced to see us, although they mourned for their companions slain by the Cyclops.

We divided among the ships the sheep we had taken from Polyphemus's flock and we sacrificed to the gods. And at dawn on the next day, we sailed away.

Odysseus Continues His Story: Circe the Enchantress

We soon came to the island where Aeolus, the lord of the winds, has his home. Aeolus treated us kindly, and asked me again and again to tell him about what had happened at Troy. When at last it was time to go, Aeolus offered to help us.

He gave me a bag made from the hide of an

ox, very thick and strong, and in that bag he put all the winds that would **hinder** us in getting home. He tied the bag shut with a silver cord and put the bag in my ship. Then he sent the west wind to blow on our sails so that we might reach our own land quickly.

hinder: get in the way of; create difficulties for

For nine days we sailed with the west wind driving us, and on the tenth day we came in sight of Ithaca, our own land. We saw the **beacon fires** on the coast. I was worn out with watching, for during all the voyage I had not closed my eyes, but had guided the ship myself and allowed no one to relieve me. But now, with home in sight, I sank down in weariness and fell into a deep sleep.

beacon fires: signal fires that can be seen at a distance

And as I slept, misfortune fell upon me. For now my men spoke together and said, "There is our native land, and we come back to it after long struggles empty-handed, while Odysseus brings gold and silver from Priam's treasure-chamber in Troy. And Aeolus has given him more treasure in that ox-hide bag. Let us take something out of that bag while he sleeps."

So they untied the mouth of the bag, and all the winds that were tied in it burst out. I woke and found that we were being driven here and there by the winds, which carried us far from our country.

The winds brought us back again to the island of Aeolus. I went to him and said, "My men have opened the bag and let all the winds fly out. And now, lord of the winds, I ask that you help me once again."

But Aeolus said to me, "Surely you are a man cursed by the gods. Leave my island, for I will not help him whom the gods hate."

We left the island of Aeolus with heavy hearts. For six days we toiled at the oars, for now there was no wind to fill our sails. At last, almost dead with **fatigue**, we sighted land. We came to anchor in a sheltered bay, surrounded by towering cliffs.

I sent three men to explore the land. But very soon two of them came running back with terror-stricken faces.

fatigue: extreme tiredness

They told me they had met a maiden, tall and strong, drawing water from a spring. She said she was the daughter of the king of that country, and offered to conduct them to her father's house.

They went with her, but when they saw her father, they were seized with terror, for he was huge and hideous to behold. He seized one of the men and tore him to pieces on the spot. Then he shouted to his people—they were **cannibals**, all of them.

cannibals: people who eat human beings

My two surviving men fled for their lives. But hardly had they finished warning us when we saw a great many of the huge man-eaters rushing along the edge of the cliffs that overlooked the harbor. They began to throw large rocks and shattered our ships in pieces. Then they swarmed down the cliffs and speared the men trying to swim ashore, as if they were fishes.

Only my ship escaped destruction. My men rowed with all their might to take us from that ill-fated shore.

We came to an island where, for two days and two nights, we saw no sign of any people living there. On the third day, I took my spear and sword and climbed a hill, and from the top of the hill I saw a great wood, and smoke rising from it. I returned to the ship and I called my comrades together.

"Friends," I said, "I do not know where we are. But I have seen smoke from the hill, so there must be someone dwelling on this island."

We decided to send part of our company to go and see if there might be people there who would help us. I divided the men into two companies, with Eurylochus in charge of one, and myself in command of the other. I shook **lots** in a helmet to see who should go and search out the island, and the lot of Eurylochus was chosen.

> **lots:** objects (such as small stones) picked by chance in order to make a choice

So Eurylochus went with two and twenty men. In the forest they came upon a house built of polished stones. All round that house, wolves and lions roamed. But as Eurylochus and his men went towards the house, these wild beasts greeted them like house dogs.

The men heard a voice within the house—the voice of a woman, singing as she worked at a loom. The men called out, and the woman came out of the dwelling. She was very fair to see. She asked the men to come inside and they went into her halls—all but Eurylochus, who stayed behind.

"Welcome, fair youths," she said, "to the halls

of Circe, daughter of the sun. Sit down while I prepare a refreshment to quench your thirst on this hot day."

So they sat down, and Circe poured wine and honey in a bowl. Then she grated cheese and barley-meal, and mixed them in the bowl. And from where he stood, Eurylochus saw that she added a single drop from a small bottle.

No sooner had they drunk the wine than she struck them with a wand, and the men turned into **swine**. Then Circe drove them out of the house and put them into pens and gave them acorns to eat.

swine: pigs

When he saw this, Eurylochus ran back through the forest and told me all that had happened. Then I took up my sword and told Eurylochus to lead me to Circe's dwelling. But in tears he begged that we sail away. "Stay here by the ship," I said, "but I must go."

I made my way through the forest, when suddenly, standing in my path, I saw a handsome youth who greeted me kindly. It was no other than the god Hermes, sent with this message to me.

"Son of Laertes," he said, "have you come to

THE ENCHANTRESS CIRCE TURNS THE CREW OF ODYSSEUS INTO SWINE.

rescue your comrades? Your men are shut up in Circe's pigpens. Do you think you can simply rush in and set them free? Stop and listen, or you will end up as they are."

He stooped down and tore up a little plant. The flower of it was white as milk, and the root was black.

"Take this," said Hermes. "It is a magic herb,

which no human hand may pluck. It will give you the power to resist all the spells of Circe. When you come to her house, she will offer you an enchanted potion—and with this herb, you may drink it, for it will do you no harm. And when she strikes you with her wand, draw your sword and spring upon her as though you were going to kill her. She will be filled with fear, for no man ever resisted her power before. Then you must make her swear that she will plot no further mischief against you."

And saying these last words, Hermes vanished.

I went on and came to the house of the enchantress. I called out, and Circe opened the shining doors and invited me in. I entered her dwelling and she brought me a golden cup of the enchanted wine. I drank but was not bewitched, for the herb protected me. Then she struck me with her wand, saying, "Go to the sty and lie there with your fellows."

And as she did, I drew my sword and sprang at her as though I would slay her. She shrank back from me and cried out, "How are you able to resist my enchantments? I thought no mortal man could so do. Truly, you must be Odysseus, for Hermes told me that one day you would come to this island. But put up your sword and let us be friendly to each other."

But I said to her, "Circe, how can we be friends when you have turned my companions into swine? I fear you have some **deceit** in your heart, and plan to do me a great mischief. Swear a mighty oath that you will not harm me."

deceit: dishonest trickery

She swore by the gods, and I put up my sword. Then the handmaidens of Circe brought out golden baskets with bread and meat, and cups of honey-tasting wine. I sat at a silver table but I had no pleasure in the food before me.

When Circe saw me sitting silent and troubled she said, "Do you think this food is enchanted? I have sworn that I will not harm you, and I shall keep my word."

And I said to her, "Circe, what man of good heart could take meat and drink while his companions are trapped as swine in pigpens? If you would have me eat and drink, first let me see my companions in their own forms."

Then Circe led the way, holding her wand in

her hand, and opened the pens and drove out the swine. She rubbed on each a magic potion, and the bristles fell from their bodies and they became men, only younger and fairer than before. And when they saw me, they wept for joy, and Circe herself was moved with pity.

"Noble Odysseus," said she, "I know how much all of you have suffered at sea, but now that is over. Stay here till you are as strong and hearty as you were when you left Ithaca, for now you are weakened both in body and mind, and have no cheer left in you."

After that we lived on Circe's island in friendship with the enchantress. Days lengthened into weeks, and weeks into months, and still we remained there. But in all of us there was a longing to return to our own land. And so I asked Circe to let us go on our homeward way.

"I will not keep you here against your will," said Circe. "You may leave, but a long journey lies before you." And she told us of the many dangers we would meet on our voyage.

Odysseus Continues His Story: Of the Sirens and Other Wonders

"First," said Circe, "you shall come to the island of the Sirens, who sit in their field of flowers and **bewitch** all men with their singing. Whoever comes too near and hears the sound of their voices—never again shall that man see home or wife or child. All round where the Sirens sit are great heaps of the bones of men. But I will tell you, Odysseus, how you may pass them.

> **bewitch:** cast a spell on

"When you come near the Sirens, put wax over the ears of your men so that none of them may hear. But if you wish to hear their song, then have your men bind you hand and foot to the ship's mast. And if you beg them to untie you, then must they bind you tighter still. When your companions have sailed the ship past where the Sirens sing, only then can they untie you.

"Once you have passed the Sirens, then you must choose which way you will take. One way takes you to the Wandering Rocks. No ship can pass them by unharmed. All around them the waves toss the **timbers** of shattered ships and the bodies of drowned men.

timbers: boards, pieces of wood

"The other way takes you between two rocks. The first rises with a sharp peak that reaches to the clouds. In the middle of it there is a cave, and that cave is the den of Scylla. She yelps with the voice of a young hound but in truth she is a terrible monster. She has six necks, and on each neck there is a hideous head, and each head has three rows of teeth. No ship ever yet got past her without losing some men, for she shoots out all her heads at once, and carries off a man in each mouth.

"Close by is the other rock, lying flat and low, with a great fig tree growing on it. Beneath it lies Charybdis. She sits there sucking down the water and spouting it forth. If you are near when she sucks the water down, then not even Poseidon's help could save you. Keep nearer to Scylla than to Charybdis, for it is better to lose six of your men than to lose them all.

"After this, you will come to an island where you will see seven herds of cattle and seven flocks of sheep. These creatures belong to the Sun, who sees everything that men do over all the earth.

These creatures neither breed nor die. If you leave these herds alone, then all of you shall return to Ithaca. But if you harm them, then your ship will be broken, and all your comrades will perish, and you shall return alone after long delay."

Having told me these things, Circe departed. I went to the ship and roused my men. Speedily we went aboard, and then a breeze filled the sails and we left the island of Circe the enchantress.

I told my companions what Circe had told me about the Sirens in their field of flowers. I took a great piece of wax and warmed it until it was soft. Then I sealed the ears of my men, and they bound me upright to the mast of the ship. The wind dropped and the sea became calm and level. So my comrades took down the sails and put out the oars.

As our ship neared their island, the Sirens lifted up their voices and began to sing a sweet and piercing song. "Come **hither**, Odysseus," the Sirens sang. "No one ever sailed past us without staying to hear our sweet song—and he who listens will go on his way a wiser man. We know all things, all the ills that the gods laid upon the Greeks at Troy, and we can

hither: here, to this place

tell you everything that is going to happen upon the earth. Odysseus, Odysseus, come to our field of flowers, and hear our song."

My heart was mad to hear the Sirens' song. I commanded my men to untie me, but they bound me even tighter, and bent to their oars and rowed on. When we had gone past the island of the Sirens, the men took the wax from their ears and released me from the mast.

No sooner had we passed the island than we heard the roaring of the sea, and the water boiled around us and the blinding spray lashed our faces. My men threw down their oars in terror. I went among them to encourage them. "Friends," I said, "this is not the first time that we have been in danger. Now, do as I say, and row with all your might."

I told them nothing of the monster Scylla, for I knew the men would lose heart if I did. And so we began to drive through a narrow strait. On one side was Scylla and on the other Charybdis. Fear gripped the men when they saw Charybdis gulping down the water so that we could see even to the sand at the bottom of the sea. But as we looked, the monster Scylla seized six of my company. As they were lifted up in the mouths of her six heads they called to me in their agony. But I could do nothing to help them. They were carried up to be devoured in the monster's den. Of all the things that I have seen upon the sea, this was the most **pitiful** of all.

> **pitiful:** heartbreaking, distressing

Having passed Scylla and Charybdis, we came near the island where the Sun keeps his herds and flocks. While we were on the ship, I heard the **lowing** of the cattle of the Sun. I spoke to my company and told them that we must steer away from the island.

> **lowing:** mooing

But this threw my men into **despair**. Eurylochus said, "It is easy for you, Odysseus, to speak like that, for you are a man of iron. But do you think we are all as strong as you? We are hungry and tired, and yet you would have us turn away from this fair island, where we could prepare a comfortable meal and find refreshing sleep. Let us stop here tonight, and tomorrow we will set sail again."

> **despair:** hopelessness

So Eurylochus spoke, and the rest of the company joined in what he said. Then I said, "You force me to give in, for you are many against one.

But swear to me a mighty oath, one and all of you, that if we go upon this island, none of you will slay the cattle of any herd."

They all swore the oath. We brought our ship to a harbor and landed near a spring of fresh water, and the men got their supper ready. They wept for their comrades that Scylla had taken, and then they slept.

The dawn came, but we found that we could not take our ship out of the harbor, for the north wind and the east wind blew a hurricane. So we stayed upon the island, and the days and the weeks went by. When the corn we had brought in the ship was all eaten, the men went through the island fishing and hunting. But they found little to ease their hunger.

One day while I slept, Eurylochus gave the men most evil **counsel**. "Rather than die of hunger," he said, "let us drive off the best cattle from the herds of the Sun. And if for doing this the gods will wreck us on the sea, let them do it. I would rather perish on the waves than die of hunger."

So they slaughtered the cattle and roasted

counsel: advice

their flesh. It was then that I awakened from my sleep. As I came down to the ship the smell of the roasting flesh came to me. I spoke angry words to my men, and told them they had done a terrible thing. And indeed the gods began at once to show us **dreadful** signs, for the hides of the cattle crawled about, and the meat, whether cooked or raw, began to low just as cows do.

> **dreadful:** causing great fear or sadness

Nevertheless, for six days my companions feasted on the cattle of the Sun. When the seventh day came, we launched our ship upon the sea and set sail.

On we sailed, but no other land appeared, and we could see only sky and sea. Zeus hung a dark cloud over us, and suddenly the west wind came fiercely down upon the ship, and the mast broke and fell on the head of the **pilot**, and he fell straight down into the sea. A thunderbolt struck the ship and all my men were swept from the deck.

> **pilot:** person who steers a ship

I never saw them again.

The west wind ceased to blow but the south wind came, and it drove the ship back towards

Selections from the Odyssey

ODYSSEUS HANGS OVER THE WHIRLPOOL CHARYBDIS.

the terrors of Scylla and Charybdis. As I neared Charybdis, my ship was sucked down. But I caught the branches of the fig tree that grew out of the rock and hung to them like a bat. There I stayed until the fragments of my ship were cast up again by Charybdis. I dropped down and caught hold of some timbers and, rowing hard with the palms of my hands, I passed the rock of Scylla without the monster seeing me.

Then for nine days I was carried along by the waves, and on the tenth day I came to the island of Calypso. Calypso took me to her dwelling and treated me kindly. But I need say no more about this, for I have told you all about it, and I hate saying the same thing over and over again.

[Here Odysseus ended the telling of his story to King Alcinous and the Phaeacians.]

Odysseus Returns to Ithaca

When Odysseus finished his tale, there was silence throughout the hall. Then King Alcinous spoke, saying, "Odysseus, we will give you a ship and we will take you to Ithaca, your own country. And now I say to those gathered here — you princes, captains, and councilors of the Phaeacians — I say that while garments and gold are already stored for Odysseus in a chest, let each of us now also give him a gift."

Pleased with this idea, each man went to his house, and the next day, when rosy-fingered dawn appeared, each carried his gift to the ship on which Odysseus was to sail.

And so Odysseus, after many thanks to the king and queen, boarded the ship. The mariners took to their oars and **hoisted** their sails, and the ship sped on like a strong sea-bird, taking Odysseus from the land of King Alcinous to the island of Ithaca.

> **hoisted:** raised with ropes and pulleys

When the bright star that signals the approach of dawn began to show, the ship drew near to Ithaca. The mariners guided the ship to a harbor near which there was a great cave. They ran the ship ashore and lifted out Odysseus, who was wrapped in a blanket and deeply asleep. Then they took the gifts that the Phaeacians had given him, and they set them by an olive tree, a little apart from the road, so that no wandering person might come upon Odysseus before he had awakened. Then they went back to their ship and departed from Ithaca for their own land.

Odysseus awakened on the beach. A mist lay

over all, and he did not know what land he had come to. As he looked around in **bewilderment**, he saw someone approaching, who looked like a king's son.

> **bewilderment:** great confusion

The one approaching him was no youth but the goddess Athena, who had made herself look like a young man. Odysseus arose and said, "Friend, you are the first man that I have seen in this land. Tell me, what land is this, and what people?"

And the young man said, "Stranger, you must have come from a long way off if you do not know what country this is. Why, even in Troy—which, they say, is very far from this land of Greece—men have heard of Ithaca."

Even as she spoke she changed from a young man into a woman tall and fair. And she said, "Do you not know me—Athena, the daughter of Zeus, who has always helped you? I would have been more often by your side, only I did not want to go openly against my brother, Poseidon, the god of the sea, whose son, Polyphemus, you blinded. "

Odysseus answered, "It is hard for a mortal man to know you, goddess, however wise he may be, for you take so many shapes. While I was at war against Troy with the other Greeks, you were always kind to me. But I have seen so little of you since the time that we took the city of Priam and set sail for our homes. Now I ask you to tell me truly, is this Ithaca that I see? For it seems to me that I have come to some other country."

Athena answered, "Never will I leave you, for indeed you are wise and **shrewd** above all others. Come now, I will show you this land, so that you may be sure in your heart."

> **shrewd:** highly perceptive; showing sharp powers of judgment

And as the goddess spoke the mist that lay on the land scattered, and Odysseus saw that he was indeed in Ithaca—he knew the harbor and the cave, and the hill covered with forest. And he knelt down on the ground and kissed the earth of his country.

"And now," said Athena, "I will help you hide these treasures that the Phaeacians gave you, and I will tell you about the dangers that await you in your own house."

They stowed everything carefully away in the cave. Then she said to him,

"There is trouble in your halls, Odysseus. You

must endure it yet a while longer. Tell no one, neither man nor woman, that you have come home again. Bear everything, and put up with every man's insults, without a word."

She told him about the suitors of his wife, who filled his halls all day, and wasted his wealth, and who intended to slay him if he should ever return. "And now," she said, "you who are always ready with a plan, think of how you will get rid of these suitors. For years your wife has answered them **craftily**, making many promises and sending them encouraging messages, but meaning the very opposite of all she says, while she **laments** your absence and awaits your return."

> **craftily:** in a clever and tricky way
> **laments:** mourns, expresses grief about

And Odysseus said to Athena, "Stand by my side, goddess, and put your courage in my heart as you did at Troy, and I will fight three hundred men!"

"I will change your appearance so that no man shall know you," said Athena. Then she covered his body with wrinkles and dimmed his shining eyes. She made his yellow hair grey and **scanty**. She clothed

> **scanty:** skimpy; of a very small amount

him in a beggar's wrap, torn and stained, and into his hands she put a beggar's staff.

"Now," she said, "the suitors shall take no notice of you, and neither your wife nor your son shall know you. Go at once to Eumaeus, the **swineherd** who is in charge of your pigs, for he is devoted to Penelope and your son, and has always been faithful to you. Stay with him and find out how things are going. I must hasten to the house of Menelaus in Sparta. There I will fetch your son Telemachus, who went there seeking news of you."

swineherd: one who tends pigs

"But," said Odysseus, "why did you not tell him about me, since you knew all? Did you want him to wander over the seas as well, and suffer all kinds of hardship while others are wasting his wealth?"

Athena answered, "Do not be troubled about him. I guided him to do these things so that people might speak well of him. Now he sits in peace and plenty in the hall of Menelaus. The suitors have put out to sea and are lying in wait for him, for they mean to kill him before he can get home. But

I think they will first find a grave themselves."

And it was then that the goddess left Odysseus in Ithaca and went to Telemachus in Sparta, and told him to leave the house of Menelaus and Helen. And it has been told how Telemachus made haste to depart, and how Menelaus and Helen gave him noble gifts in parting.

And Telemachus, onboard the ship taking him from Sparta back to Ithaca, remained **mindful** of a warning that Athena had spoken to him: "Son of Odysseus," said she, "in returning to Ithaca, your life is in peril, for the suitors have discovered that you have gone. Two of them, Antinous and Eurymachus, are greatly angered. And Antinous, in a ship with twenty men, lies in wait for you in the strait by Ithaca, where he intends to kill you before you come again to your home. Therefore keep your ship far from that place. And when you come to the land of Ithaca, send your ship and company to the city, but go yourself to the swineherd Eumaeus, for he has always been true to you."

mindful: aware

Odysseus and the Swineherd

As for Odysseus, he obeyed the goddess Athena and, in the **guise** of an old beggar, made his way to where Eumaeus the swineherd lived, a lonely place in the hills. There, Eumaeus had enclosed a wide space of ground with a stone fence, and within the fence there were twelve pens, and in each pen there were fifty swine. Old Eumaeus lived in this place tending the swine with three young men to help him. The swine-pens were guarded by four dogs, very large and fierce.

> **guise:** external appearance (usually concealing one's true appearance)

When Odysseus approached, the dogs ran at him. He dropped his staff and sat quietly on the ground. Eumaeus heard the barking and came out of his house and drove the dogs away.

Seeing before him an ancient beggar, Eumaeus said, "Old man, the dogs might have killed you. That would have been a great grief to me, and I have grief enough already. My lord has gone away, and no one knows where he is. And while I fatten hogs for others to eat, he may be wandering in hunger through some friendless city. But come into my house, old man, and tell me your story."

So Odysseus went into the house, and the swineherd invited him to sit down on a heap of **brushwood** covered with a shaggy goat-skin.

> **brushwood:** twigs and branches, used to start a fire

"May the gods reward you for your kindness to a stranger," said Odysseus.

Eumaeus the swineherd answered, "It would be wicked not to be kind to a stranger. But I have little to give. If my master had stayed at home, I would be better off. He would have given me a house and land. Good masters—and indeed, Odysseus was a good master—give such gifts to servants who serve them well. And I have served him well. But my master will not return."

Then he prepared a meal, and Odysseus ate and drank. Not a word did he say, for he was thinking how he might punish the suitors who were wasting his goods.

At last Odysseus said, "Friend, who was this master of yours, who you say has been absent from his home so long? Perhaps I have seen him, for I have wandered over many lands."

Eumaeus the swineherd answered, "Oh, that

is what all the travelers say, but we hear no truth from them. There is not a wanderer comes here but our lady Penelope sends for him and must ask him questions, hoping that he will have something to tell her of her lord, Odysseus. And as he tells her some tale of having seen or heard of him, she weeps all the while. And you too, old man, for a shirt and a cloak, would doubtless make up a very pretty story. But as for Odysseus, no matter what the wanderers or **vagrants** say, he will never return. The wolves and birds of prey have long since torn his body to pieces, or the fishes of the sea have eaten him, and his bones are lying buried deep in the sand on some far-off shore. Never again shall I find so good a lord."

vagrants: wandering beggars

"My friend," replied Odysseus, "I tell you that Odysseus will return, and in this same year. And when this happens, you shall give me a gift such as men give to those who bring them good news—a shirt and a cloak, if you will. But till my words come true, I will take nothing from you. I hate the man who tells lies because he is poor. I would sooner die than do such a thing myself. But as sure as the old moon **wanes** and the young moon is born, Odysseus will return, and he will take vengeance on those who waste his wealth and dishonor his wife and son."

> **wanes:** grows smaller (or appears to)

"Old man," said Eumaeus the swineherd, "you will never get that shirt and cloak from me, nor will Odysseus ever come home. Drink your wine in peace, and let us talk about something else. It pains me when anyone speaks about my honored master."

When morning came, Odysseus said, "I am going to the city to beg, so that I am no longer a **burden** to you. I will go to the house of Odysseus and see if I can earn a little from the suitors who are there. I could serve them by kindling a fire or carving meat or pouring wine."

> **burden:** a load; a heavy responsibility

"No," said Eumaeus, "do not go there. Stay until Telemachus, the son of Odysseus, returns, and he will do something for you. The suitors will not welcome such a one as you to serve them. It is better that you stay here."

Odysseus did not go to the city but stayed all day with Eumaeus. And at night, when he and Eumaeus and the younger swineherds were seated at the fire, Odysseus asked Eumaeus to tell him of his own life. So they passed much of the night, with Eumaeus telling of his own wanderings and his sorrows.

And while they were speaking, Telemachus, the son of Odysseus, came to Ithaca in his good ship. Antinous waited **in ambush** for him, but Telemachus, who had been **forewarned** by the goddess Athena, arrived without being seen by his enemies. And now, having arrived at Ithaca, Telemachus told his comrades to steer the ship to the city while he himself made his way to the dwelling of the servant he trusted most—the dwelling of Eumaeus the swineherd.

in ambush: hidden in order to make a sneak attack

forewarned: told about a coming danger

Odysseus and Telemachus

In the morning, the swineherd and Odysseus kindled a fire and were making breakfast when Odysseus heard the sound of footsteps approaching the hut. The fierce dogs were outside, and he expected to hear them yelping, but they made no

EUMAEUS IS SURPRISED AND DELIGHTED BY THE RETURN OF TELEMACHUS. ODYSSEUS DOES NOT REVEAL HIMSELF TO HIS SON.

sound. "Here comes some comrade or friend," he said, "for the dogs do not bark."

As he spoke, Telemachus entered the doorway, with the dogs rubbing at his knees. When Eumaeus saw the young man, he dropped the bowl from his hand and ran to him and kissed his head and his hands. As a father kisses his only son coming back to him from a far country after long years, so did the swineherd kiss Telemachus, and spoke fondly to him.

"So," said Eumaeus, "you have come home, Telemachus! When I heard you had gone to Pylos I thought I would never see you again. Come in, dear child, and sit down. It is not very often you come into the country to see us herdsmen. I suppose you think it better to stay in the city to keep an eye on what the suitors are doing."

"So it is, old friend," answered Telemachus. "But I have come now because I want to see you, and to learn whether my mother is still in the house of Odysseus, or whether one of the suitors has taken her as a wife to his own house."

"Your mother is still in your father's house," replied Eumaeus, "grieving and weeping, night and day."

Odysseus rose to give Telemachus his seat but the young man said, "Be seated, friend. I can easily find another seat."

Eumaeus spread a **fleece** upon some brushwood and Telemachus seated himself. Then the swineherd hurried to feed his new guest. He prepared a meal of cold meat, the remains from what they had eaten the day before, and he filled baskets with bread and poured wine into wooden bowls.

> **fleece:** a soft wooly sheepskin

When they had had enough to eat and drink, Telemachus said to Eumaeus, "Old friend, where does this stranger come from?"

"He has wandered through many countries," said Eumaeus, "and has come here seeking help. I have done what I can for him, and now I hand him to you to do with as you will."

Telemachus said, "How can I support any man? I do not have the strength to defend my own house. But I will do what I can for this stranger. I will give him a cloak and shirt, with shoes for his feet and a sword to defend himself, and I will send him on whatever way he wants to go. But, Eumaeus, I would not have him go near my father's house. The suitors grow more insolent each day, and they might **mock** the stranger if he went among them."

> **mock:** tease in a mean way

Odysseus, who had not seen his son since he was an infant, desired to learn something more of his mind and character, and so he said, "I am shocked at what you have said about these insolent suitors. Tell me, do you allow such behavior in your own father's house? And what about your brothers? Surely, a man may look to them for support, however great his **quarrel** may be. I wish I were as young as you. I would rather die fighting in my own house than see such shameful things done day after day."

quarrel: argument, disagreement

Telemachus answered, "The suitors of my mother are powerful men, and the people fear them. And as for brothers, I have none, grandfather, Laertes, had but one son, Odysseus, and Odysseus had none other but me. And so these suitors make **havoc** in my household, and, it may be, will take my life also. These things, however, are in the hands of the gods."

havoc: destruction and disorder

Then Telemachus turned to Eumaeus and said, "Old friend, go and tell my mother that I am safe and have returned. Tell it to her alone, and then come back here without letting anyone else know, for there are many who are plotting evil against me."

Eumaeus at once took his staff in his hands and started toward the city. Telemachus lay down and closed his eyes in weariness. He saw, while thinking that he only dreamt it, a woman come to the gate. She was tall and splendid, and the dogs shrank away from her with a whine. She touched the beggar with a golden wand. As she did, the marks of age and beggary fell from him and the man stood up, tall and noble-looking.

Telemachus started up and saw the man standing before him. "Who are you?" cried Telemachus. "A moment ago you seemed an aged beggar, and now you look like a chief of men! Are you one of the divine gods?'

Odysseus looked upon him and said, "I am no god. I am your father. After much suffering and much wandering I have come to my own country." He kissed his son with tears flowing down his cheeks, and Telemachus threw his arms around his father's neck, almost afraid to believe that the father he had searched for was indeed before him.

But all doubt vanished as Odysseus talked to

him and told him how the Phaeacians had brought him to Ithaca, and how he had many gifts that were hidden in the cave, and how Athena had changed his appearance into that of an old beggar. And when his story was finished Odysseus said, "Come, my son, tell me of the suitors who waste the substance of our house. Tell me how many of them there are, and who they are, so that we may prepare a way of dealing with them."

"Even though you are a great warrior, my father," said Telemachus, "you and I on our own cannot hope to deal with them. They come not just from Ithaca but from all the islands around. We two cannot deal with such a **throng**."

> **throng:** crowd

Odysseus replied, "I will make a plan to deal with them. Go home, and keep company with the suitors. Later in the day the swineherd will lead me into the city, and I will go into the house in the likeness of an old beggar. And if you see any of the suitors mistreat me, harden your heart to endure it. Even if they drag me by the feet to the door of the house, keep quiet. And let no one know that Odysseus has returned—not even your mother,

Penelope, nor my father, Laertes."

Telemachus said, "My father, you shall soon learn what spirit is in me and what wisdom I have."

In the afternoon, Eumaeus came back to the hut. Athena had again given Odysseus the appearance of an ancient beggar, and so the swineherd saw no change in his guest.

The Beggar in the House of Odysseus

The next day, Telemachus took his spear in his hand and said to the swineherd, "Eumaeus, my friend, I will go to the city, for my mother will not rest till she sees my face. You will take the stranger with you, so that he may beg of any that may be willing to give."

"Yes," said Odysseus in the guise of a beggar, "that is what I want. If a man must beg, it is better to beg in the city than in the country."

So Telemachus returned to the city. When he went into his house, the first person he saw was his nurse, old Eurycleia, who welcomed him with joy. Then Penelope came out of her room and flung her arms about her son. "Light of my eyes," she cried as she kissed his forehead, "you are home. I was sure I was never going to see you again. Come, tell me what you saw."

Telemachus gave her a brief account of his visit to Nestor and Menelaus, and then said, "Dear mother, you will hear all in time, but at present I have other work to do. Go now and pray to the gods to grant us our revenge upon the suitors. I will return soon."

Penelope did as her son asked. She washed her face, changed her dress, and went upstairs with her handmaidens to pray for revenge upon the suitors.

At that time Odysseus and Eumaeus were journeying towards the city. Odysseus had a **ragged** bag across his shoulders and he carried a staff to help him over the slippery ground.

ragged: old and torn

They paused to rest at a fountain near the city wall, and there they came across a servant from Odysseus's house, a goatherd named Melanthius. He was leading a flock of goats for the suitors to kill, and when he saw the swineherd with his companion he cried out to Eumaeus, "Now we see the **vile** leading the vile. Why do you bring beggars to the city? We have enough of them already." And he kicked Odysseus, thinking to knock him over.

But Odysseus stood firm and **considered** whether he should strike the fellow with his staff or fling him on the ground. In the end, he hardened his heart to endure the insult, and let the goatherd go on his way.

> **vile:** extremely unpleasant, disgusting
>
> **considered:** thought carefully before making a decision

They journeyed onward and soon came near the great house of Odysseus. And as they entered the courtyard, there lay a dog, Argos by name, which had belonged to Odysseus years ago. All uncared for he lay in the dirt, old and feeble. He had once been a famous hound, and Odysseus himself had trained him before he went to the wars of Troy. But now he was old and no one looked after him.

When the dog saw his old master, he knew him at once, and wagged his tail and drooped his ears, and struggled to get up from the place where he lay. When Odysseus saw him, the tears came into his eyes, and he said to the swineherd, "Now this is strange, Eumaeus, that so good a dog should lie here uncared for in the dirt."

The swineherd answered, "He belongs to a master who died far away from his home. Once there was no dog faster or stronger. But his master is dead, and now no one cares for him."

The dog had waited twenty years for his master to appear, and now, he had seen him at last. And the dog lay down his head and died.

Odysseus and the swineherd approached the house. Behind the swineherd, Odysseus stepped into his own hall in the appearance of a ragged beggar leaning on a staff. Odysseus looked upon the young lords who wooed his wife, and then he sat down upon the **threshold** and went no further into the hall.

threshold: the bottom of a doorway that one crosses in entering a house or room

Telemachus was there. Seeing Eumaeus, he took a loaf from the breadbasket and as much meat as he could hold. He gave these to the swineherd, saying, "Give this food to the stranger at the doorway, and tell him that he may go among the company and ask **alms** from each."

alms: money or food given to help the poor

Odysseus ate while the minstrel was finishing

a song. As the song ended, Odysseus rose up and wandered around the room, stretching out his hand as beggars do, and many of the suitors gave him something.

But Antinous, the most insolent of the suitors, cried out, "Swineherd, why have you brought this fellow here? Have we not beggars enough already to bother us?"

Hearing this speech from Antinous, Telemachus said, "Antinous, we are not so poor that we need to drive the stranger from our doors. Take something and give it to him yourself—but you were always better at taking than giving."

"Telemachus," replied Antinous, "what do you mean by this bold talk? I will give the beggar something that will keep him from the house for three months to come." And as he spoke he grabbed a heavy footstool from under the table and waved it as though he would throw it at Odysseus.

But Odysseus came up to him and spoke. "They say you are the noblest of all the suitors," he said, "and for that reason you should give me a better thing than any of the others have given me. Look upon me. I too was a rich man once, and had a fine house of my own. In those days I gave to many a wanderer such as I am now, no matter who he might be."

"Get away from my table, you miserable pest," said Antinous.

Then Odysseus replied, "Lord Antinous, you have a fair face but a **foul** heart. Here you sit at another man's table and yet you cannot find it in your heart to give something out of the plenty that is before you."

> **foul:** wicked, offensive

At these words, Antinous grabbed the footstool and with it he struck Odysseus on the back, at the base of the right shoulder. Such a blow would have knocked another man over, but Odysseus stood firm as a rock under it.

He gave one look at Antinous, and then went over and sat down again in the doorway of the hall. And he said to those who sat feasting in the hall, "Hear me, you suitors of the queen! Antinous has struck me because I am poor. I say, if the poor have gods willing to avenge them, then may they bring Antinous to a bad end before the day of his marriage."

Antinous angrily shouted, "Be silent, stranger! Or I will have you dragged from the house and the flesh torn from your bones."

But even the suitors blamed him. One of the young men said, "Antinous, you were wrong to strike the stranger. Do you not know that sometimes the gods take the shape of poor beggars, and visit the dwellings of men to test whether they are good or bad?" But Antinous did not care.

As for Telemachus, he was full of anger but he kept it to himself. He did not shed a tear nor did he speak a word, but he thought of the time when the suitors would suffer for all their wrongdoings.

When Penelope heard of how Antinous treated the stranger, she prayed that the gods might strike down the wicked man. Then she sent for Eumaeus, and said to him, "Bring this stranger to me. I want to talk with him. Perhaps he has heard something of Odysseus, or has even seen him, for I hear that he has wandered far."

Eumaeus answered, "Indeed, my queen, he does say that he has heard of Odysseus."

"Call him here, then," said Penelope, "that I

too may hear his story. And if I am satisfied that the stranger is speaking the truth, I shall give him a good shirt and cloak to wear."

Then Eumaeus went to Odysseus and told him of the queen's wish to speak with him. But Odysseus did not think that the time had yet come to let his wife know who he was, and he suspected that if he went to talk to her, she would see through his disguise. So he said to the swineherd, "I am more than willing to tell the truth about Odysseus to the fair and wise Penelope. I would gladly tell the queen all that I know about her husband. But I am afraid of these wicked young suitors. Tell the queen, therefore, that if she will wait till the evening, when the suitors have gone, then I will speak to her. And ask her to give me a seat near the fire, so that I may sit and warm myself as I speak."

Then the swineherd went back to the queen. And when she saw that the beggar was not with him she said, "Why have you not brought him?"

The swineherd answered, "My lady, he asks that you wait till the evening, after those **haughty** and

haughty: proud in a mean and stuck-up way

violent young men have left, and then you can speak with him alone."

Penelope said, "The stranger is wise, and it shall be as he says."

Then Eumaeus the swineherd went back to the hall and whispered to Telemachus, "I am going back to the farm, to look after things there. Take care of yourself. There are many here who are ready to do you harm. May the gods bring them to a bad end!"

Telemachus answered, "Go, old friend, and come again tomorrow."

So the swineherd went away, and the suitors continued to feast and make merry as Odysseus sat in the guise of a beggar on the threshold of his own house.

Penelope and the Stranger

While these things were happening, Penelope called to the old nurse Eurycleia and said, "I will go into the hall of our house. I will speak to the suitors, though they are as hateful to me as ever."

The old woman suggested, "Dear lady, first

wash your face. Do not let the tears be seen on your cheeks."

But the queen said, "What do I care how I look, now that my husband is gone? But tell two of my handmaidens to come with me, for I would not go among these men alone."

So old Eurycleia went to tell the handmaidens. But Athena would not let the queen have her own way in this matter. The goddess caused a deep sleep to fall upon her, and as Penelope slept, Athena bathed her face and took all weariness away from her body, and restored her youthfulness. And when Penelope came among the suitors with her two handmaidens, one standing on each side of her, the hearts of all were enchanted with love for her, and each hoped that she might be his wife.

One of the suitors, Eurymachus by name, came forward and spoke to Penelope, saying, "Lady, so fair are you, indeed above all the women in the land."

Penelope replied, "Do not talk to me of beauty. My beauty departed in the grief I felt when my lord went to the wars of Troy. I remember how, when he left, he took me by the hand, and said,

'O lady, I do not know whether I shall come back to my home or perish there before the walls of Troy. Therefore, care for my father and for my mother while I am away. And bring up our son, Telemachus. And when he is a bearded man, then, if I am dead, marry whom you will. So my husband said.'"

Penelope paused, and all the suitors listened as she spoke again. "And now the time is come, for he is dead. It is ten years since Troy was taken, and yet he has not come back, and Telemachus is grown to be a man, and I must marry again, although I am unhappy. And I have yet another trouble. My suitors are not like the suitors of other women. For the custom is that when a man wishes to marry a lady, he brings gifts of sheep and oxen and makes a feast for his kindred and friends. My suitors, however, bring nothing. Instead, they take what I have, and offer nothing in return."

When he heard this **artful** speech of Penelope, Odysseus smiled to himself, for he saw her intention, which was to draw gifts from the suitors, and raise their hopes that she would soon choose one of them to marry, even as

> **artful:** clever, crafty

she hated them in her heart.

And her plan succeeded. Antinous said, "Lady, we will give you gifts. But we will not depart from this place till you have chosen one of us for your husband."

Each suitor sent a servant to fetch his gift. Antinous gave a splendid embroidered robe with twelve golden clasps, another gave a necklace of amber and gold, and another a pair of jeweled earrings.

Then the queen went back to her room upstairs, and her maids brought these and many other gifts after her. Meanwhile the suitors took to singing and dancing, and stayed till evening came. And as darkness fell they lit torches in the hall.

As Odysseus in his beggar's rags stood near one of the torches, the suitor Eurymachus laughed and called out, "How fortunate that the gods have sent this man to us. See how the torchlight flashes on his bald head!" And he turned to Odysseus and said, "Stranger, will you work as a hired servant at my farm among the hills? Can you build a stone fence or plant trees? If so, you shall have clothes, and shoes for your feet, and bread to eat. But no, it seems you have got into bad ways, and do not want to work. You would rather fill your belly by begging."

Odysseus said to the **scornful** suitor, "Lord Eurymachus, you think yourself a great man. But if Odysseus should return, that door, wide as it is, would be too narrow for your escape."

> **scornful:** full of disrespect

"You dog!" cried Eurymachus, and in fury he lifted a footstool to fling at Odysseus. But Telemachus cried out, "That man must not be struck again in this hall. Sirs, if you have finished feasting, go to your own homes. Go now, and in peace."

All were surprised to hear Telemachus speak so boldly. No one answered him back. Then one of the suitors said, "Ever since that beggar came here, there has been quarrelling. We shall have no more pleasure in the feast tonight, so let each man go to his home." And they agreed and left for the night.

When the suitors had gone, Odysseus said to Telemachus, "My son, we must now take the weapons out of this hall. Remove them from the walls."

From the walls where the weapons hung, Telemachus and his father took down the helmets and shields and sharp-pointed spears. As they carried them out, Odysseus said, "Tomorrow, if the suitors ask why the weapons have been moved, say that you have moved them away from the smoke of the fire, which has dulled them so that they no longer shine like the weapons that Odysseus left behind when he went to the wars of Troy."

So Telemachus and his father carried the spears and swords and shields from the hall to a storeroom. And when they had finished, Odysseus said to the young man, "Go now to your room and rest. I wish to talk to your mother."

And soon Penelope came to the hall to speak to the stranger. To the old nurse who had come with her, Penelope said, "Eurycleia, bring a bench to the fire, with a fleece upon it, so this stranger may sit and tell me his story."

Eurycleia brought over the bench, and Odysseus sat down near the fire. Then Penelope said, "First, stranger, tell me who you are. What was your father's name, and from what country do you come?"

Odysseus answered, "Lady, ask me what you will, but not my name or my country. To think of these brings tears to my eyes, and I do not want anyone to see me weeping."

Penelope said, "I too have had many sorrows and have shed many tears since the day when my husband left me, joining the Greeks to fight against the men of Troy. So many troubles have come upon me! For the princes of this island of Ithaca, and of the other islands round about, come here asking me to marry. And they sit here day after day, and eat up the wealth of this house, and I do not know how to escape them. For years, indeed, I put them off, for I said that I could not marry till I had woven a shroud for my husband's father. And I worked at weaving this shroud in the day, and at night I undid the weaving. But one of the maids told the suitors what I did, and now I cannot devise any other plan to keep marriage away from me. My father and mother urge me to marry, while my son sees these suitors consuming the wealth that should be his. And there is no reason why I should not be wed again, for surely Odysseus, my husband, is dead."

Odysseus said, "I knew your husband. On his way to Troy he came to my land, for the wind blew him out of his course. I gave food and wine to him and to his people. Twelve days they stayed, for the wind blew from the north and hindered their sailing, but on the thirteenth day it blew from the south, and they departed."

When Penelope heard this, her heart melted and tears ran down her cheeks. Odysseus had pity for his wife. Tears would have run down his own cheeks as well, but he forced himself to hold them back.

Odysseus said, "Weep no more, lady. Do not think of your lord as if he were dead. I swear that Odysseus himself will stand here before the old moon wanes and the new moon is born."

Penelope said, "May your words come true, old man. But wanderers have told me such comforting things before, and so I have many doubts. Now the maids will make a bed for you with a mattress and blankets, so that you may sleep warmly till the morning. And they shall wash your feet."

Odysseus said, "I thank you, lady, but I need no blankets or mattress. I do not care for these things, for it is long since I have used them. But if there is some old woman among your servants, one whom you trust, who will wash my feet, then let her do so, if you will allow it."

Penelope said, "There is such a woman in the house. She nursed my husband, and cared for him, and carried him in her arms, ever since he was born. She is weak with old age, yet still she can wash your feet."

So the queen called the old nurse Eurycleia, and said to her, "Come, nurse, wash this stranger's feet. He is one that knows your master Odysseus."

Old Eurycleia fetched water, both hot and cold. And standing before Odysseus in the flickering light of the fire, she said, "I will wash your feet, for Penelope's sake and for your own. And also because you are like him — many strangers have come here, but I never saw one that was so like Odysseus as you are."

His feet were in the water, and she put her hand upon one of them. As she did so, Odysseus turned his face away to the darkness, for it suddenly came into his mind that his nurse, old Eurycleia, might recognize the scar that was upon his foot.

The scar had been made long ago when Odysseus, then a youth, had gone hunting, and a mighty boar charged at him, and the boar's tusk ripped deep into the flesh of his foot. And now, as Eurycleia, his old nurse, passed her hands along the leg, she let his foot drop suddenly. His knee struck against the **vessel** of water and it overturned. The nurse touched the chin of Odysseus and she gasped, "It is you—you are Odysseus."

> **vessel:** a container to hold liquid

She looked to where Penelope was sitting so that she might tell her, but Penelope had her eyes turned away, sitting like one in a dream, lost in memories. Odysseus put his hand over Eurycleia's mouth, and with the other hand he drew her to him.

"Nurse," he whispered, "be silent. I have come back after these twenty years, but no one must know till I have got all things ready."

"Silent I'll be," said the old nurse Eurycleia. "I will hold my tongue like a stone or a piece of iron. By no sign will I let anyone know that you have come under this roof."

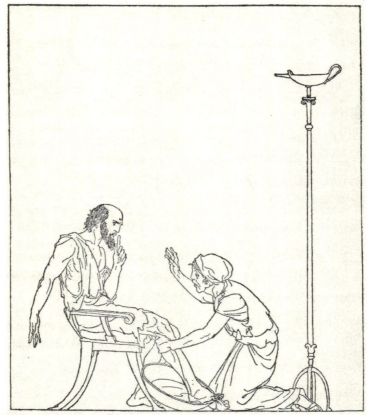

SEEING THE SCAR, EURYCLEIA KNOWS THAT THE BEGGAR IS REALLY ODYSSEUS, BUT HE MAKES HER PROMISE NOT TO REVEAL HIS SECRET.

She went out of the hall to fetch more water, and then came back and finished bathing his feet. Then Odysseus arranged the rags around his leg to hide the scar, and he drew the bench closer to the fire.

Penelope turned to him again. "Stranger," she said, "I would tell you of a dream I dreamt. I thought that I saw a flock of geese, and that a great eagle came swooping down from a mountain and dug his curved beak into the neck of each of them till he had killed them all. And then the eagle spoke to me in the voice of a man, saying, 'This is no dream but a true vision. The geese are the suitors, and I that appeared as an eagle am your husband who will swiftly bring death to them.' Then the dream went away, and I wakened and looked out on the daylight and saw my geese in the yard pecking at the ground. Can you tell me what this dream means?"

"Lady," said Odysseus, "the meaning is as the dream says. The death of the suitors is coming, and not a single one of them will escape."

"Ah," said Penelope, "it is hard to tell false dreams from true. But now the day of my woe is at hand. I am being forced to choose a husband from the suitors, and depart from the house of Odysseus."

"And how will you choose from among them?" said Odysseus.

"In this way," said Penelope. "I will hold a trial of strength and skill. My husband's great bow is still here in the house. He used to set up twelve axes, all lined up in a row, one behind another. Then he would walk away from them and bend his bow and shoot an arrow through the holes in the backs of the twelve axes. I shall make the suitors try to do the same thing. The one who can bend the bow and send his arrow through all twelve axes — him will I choose for my husband."

Odysseus said, "Your plan is a good one. And do not delay this contest of the bow any longer. Let it be tomorrow."

"Stranger," said Penelope, "I thank you for your counsel. And now goodnight, for I must go to my rest."

So Penelope went to her chamber with her handmaidens. And in her bed she thought over all that the stranger had told her of Odysseus, and she wept again for her husband, until Athena poured sweet sleep over her eyelids.

The Trial of the Bow and the Revenge of Odysseus

Odysseus lay down but he could not sleep, for he was thinking about many things—especially how he, being but one man, with perhaps two or three to help him, could slay all the suitors.

While he turned from side to side, Athena came to him and said, "Why do you not sleep? Here you are in your own home, and you find that your wife is true to you, and that your son is just as you could wish. What troubles you?"

Odysseus answered, "What you say, goddess, is true. But I keep thinking how I, being one against many, will be able to slay the suitors. This troubles me."

The goddess answered, "The gods are on your side; I am with you, and will stay by you to the end." And she poured sleep on his eyes, and left him.

In the morning, Odysseus went outside and looked up to the sky. "O Zeus," he said, "send me a sign that, in bringing me back to my country, you mean to do me good." There came thunder from the sky, and Odysseus was glad to hear it.

Then Melanthius the goatherd came, bringing goats for the day's feast. When he saw Odysseus, he spoke roughly to him. "Old man," he said, "are you still pestering us with your begging? Are there no other feasts you can go to?"

Odysseus made no answer, but only bowed his head.

Then Eumaeus the swineherd came, driving three fat hogs for the day's feast, followed by the cowherd, whose name was Philoetius. He was bringing a calf for the feast. When he saw Odysseus in the guise of a beggar, he called out to him, "Friend, I hope that you may have better luck in the time to come, for I see that you now have many troubles. You make me think of my master Odysseus, who even now may be as you are, dressed in rags and wandering in friendless lands. I take care of his cattle, and they have increased under my hand, but it disturbs me to see these strangers devouring them in his own home. I would have run away long ago to serve in some other house, except that I hope my poor master might yet return and send all these suitors flying."

Odysseus said to him, "I see that you are a good man, and I swear that this day, you shall see Odysseus with your own eyes—and the end of the suitors as well."

And now the suitors came and sat down to their morning meal. Odysseus stood outside the hall until Telemachus came and brought him inside.

By this time Penelope had gone with a servant to the treasure-chamber in which Odysseus's great bow was kept. She thrust the bronze key into the locks, and pulled at the doors, which groaned as a bull groans. She went inside and saw the great bow upon its peg. She took it down and laid it upon her knees, and thought of the man who had bent it.

Beside the bow was its **quiver** full of bronze-weighted arrows. The servant took the quiver and Penelope took the bow, and they went to the hall where the suitors were feasting.

> **quiver:** a case for holding arrows

Penelope spoke to the men, saying, "Hear me, you lords of Ithaca and of the islands around—you who come here day after day, claiming that you wish to marry me. The time has come for me to make my choice of a man from among you. Here is how I shall make my choice."

She grasped the great bow and said, "This is the bow of Odysseus, my lord who is no more. Whoever among you who can bend this bow and shoot an arrow from it through the holes in the backs of twelve axes lined up in a row, him will I take for my husband."

As she spoke Telemachus set twelve axes upright in an even line, so that one could shoot an arrow through the hole in the back of each axehead. Then Eumaeus, the old swineherd, took the bow of Odysseus and laid it before the suitors.

One of the suitors took up the bow and tried to bend it, but he could not. Then others took the bow and warmed it at the fire, and rubbed the bowstring with fat, trying to soften it. Still they could not bend it. One after another they tried, but **in vain**, till only two were left, Antinous and Eurymachus, who were indeed the strongest of them all.

in vain: unsuccessfully

As the suitors were trying to bend the bow, Eumaeus the swineherd and Philoetius the cowherd stepped out of the hall. Odysseus followed them and laid a hand on each and said, "Swineherd and cowherd, I have a word to say to you. But will you keep it to yourselves? First, what would you do to help Odysseus if he should return? Would you stand on his side, or on the side of the suitors? Answer me now from your hearts."

Philoetius the cowherd said, "May Zeus grant my wish and bring Odysseus back! Then you will know on whose side I stand." And Eumaeus said, "If Odysseus should return, I would be on his side with all the strength that is in me."

Odysseus said, "Then know that I am your master, Odysseus. After twenty years I have come back to my own country. If you need to see a sign that I am indeed Odysseus, look down on my foot. See there the mark that the wild boar left on me in the days of my youth."

Eumaeus and Philoetius looked down, and the swineherd and the cowherd saw the scar and knew it well. Knowing that it was indeed Odysseus who stood before them, they cast their arms around him and kissed him on the head and shoulders. And Odysseus was moved by their tears, and he kissed their heads and their hands.

As they went back to the hall, Odysseus said to Eumaeus, "After the suitors have tried the bow, bring it to me." He told him also to order Eurycleia, the faithful nurse, to bar the doors of the women's room, and to tell the women not to come into the hall, even if they should hear the noise of battle. To Philoetius the cowherd he said, "Lock the doors of the hall, and fasten them with a rope."

As Odysseus went into the hall, one of the suitors, Eurymachus, was struggling to bend the bow. "Woe is me!" he groaned. "I am grieved, though not for the loss of this marriage—there are other women in Greece—but because we are all weaker than the great Odysseus. This is, indeed, a shameful thing."

Then Antinous, the proudest of the suitors, said, "Do not lose heart. It does not please the god of **archers** to favor us this day, but we will try again tomorrow."

archers: people skilled in shooting bows and arrows

Then Odysseus came forward and said, "Sirs, let me try it. I want to know whether I still have the strength I had when I was young."

All the suitors were very angry that the ragged

stranger should dare to think of such a thing. Antinous spoke sharply and said, "You **wretched** beggar! Is it not enough that we let you pick up scraps, and now you must force your way into our conversation? **Begone**, or we will have you cut into pieces."

> **wretched:** miserable
> **begone:** go away

Then Penelope said, "Antinous, it is not right that you should ill-treat any guest of Telemachus who comes to this house. The man should be allowed to try if he can bend the bow."

And Telemachus said, "Mother, if it pleases me that this stranger shall try it, then it shall be so, and no man shall say otherwise. But now, you and your maids go to your rooms; these things are for men to settle."

Telemachus said this because he knew what would soon happen in the hall, and he did not want his mother there. She wondered to hear him speak with such authority, but she made no protest. She turned and went out of the hall, taking her handmaidens with her.

Then Telemachus gave the bow to Eumaeus the swineherd and told him to take it to the beggar. The suitors raised angry cries, but they did not stop the swineherd as he took the bow to Odysseus. And when Eumaeus had done this, he went to the old nurse Eurycleia and told her to keep the women behind their doors whatever they might hear. And Philoetius the cowherd went out of the hall and barred the gates leading out of the courtyard.

Odysseus stood in the doorway of the hall with the bow in his hands and with the arrows scattered at his feet. He handled it as a minstrel handles a lyre when he stretches a cord or tightens a peg. Then he bent the great bow; he bent it without an effort, and at his touch the bow-string made a sound that was like the cry of a swallow. Seeing him bend that mighty bow, each and every suitor felt a sharp pain at the heart. They saw Odysseus take up an arrow and fit it to the string. He held the notch, and he drew the string, and he shot the bronze-weighted arrow straight through the holes in the back of the axe heads.

Then he said, "You see, my lord Telemachus, that your guest does not shame you through foolish boasting. I have bent the bow of Odysseus,

ODYSSEUS SHOOTS AN ARROW THROUGH THE AXE HEADS.

and the arrow flew straight and true."

Saying this, he nodded to Telemachus, who instantly took his sword and spear in his hand. Outside, the thunder of Zeus rumbled.

"But now," said Odysseus, "before the sun goes down, there is yet another feast to serve to these suitors." As he spoke, he aimed an arrow at Antinous. The man was raising a cup of wine to his lips. There was not a thought of danger in his mind, for who could dream that any man, no matter how strong or brave, would dare such a thing, being but one against many? The head of the arrow passed through the neck of Antinous, and the blood gushed out of his nostrils, and he fell dead across the table.

When they saw him fall, for a moment the suitors doubted whether the stranger had killed the man by chance or on purpose. Then they leapt from their seats, eagerly seeking the weapons on the walls, but when they looked, they saw that all the arms had been taken down.

Then Odysseus shouted, "You dogs, that said in your hearts that Odysseus would never return to his home! You that have wasted my wealth, and troubled my wife, and injured my servants, having no fear of god or man! Behold Odysseus returned, and know that a sudden destruction has come upon you all."

They turned pale with fear as he spoke, and every man looked round to see where he might run for safety. Then Eurymachus said, "If you are indeed Odysseus of Ithaca, then it is true that we have done you great wrong. But the man who was most to blame lies here dead. It was Antinous who was the chief of your enemies. He wanted not merely to marry your wife but also to destroy your house, and to be king of Ithaca. But we will pay you back twenty times for all that we have taken of yours."

Odysseus said, "Do not talk to me of payment. You shall pay me with your lives, every one of you."

Then Eurymachus shouted out, "Friends, this man will not stop till he has killed us all. We must fight him. Draw your swords and hold up the tables to shield you from his arrows."

As he spoke, he rushed on with his two-edged knife in his hand. But Odysseus, with a terrible cry, shot an arrow that pierced Eurymachus through the breast. The blade fell from his hand, and he fell forward dead.

One of the suitors rushed straight at Odysseus with his sword, but Telemachus drove his spear through this man's shoulders. Then Telemachus ran quickly to the room where the weapons and armor were stored. The swineherd and the cowherd joined him, and all three put on armor. Odysseus, as long as he had arrows to defend himself, kept shooting at the suitors, striking them down. When all the arrows were gone, he put the helmet on his head, and took up the shield and two great spears that Telemachus had brought.

But now Melanthius, the goatherd who was the enemy of Odysseus, got into the storeroom where the arms were kept. He brought out spears and shields and helmets, and gave them to the suitors. Seeing the goatherd go back for more arms, Telemachus and Eumaeus followed him. They caught him and bound him with a rope. Then they hastened back to the hall and stood by the side of Odysseus.

One suitor grabbed a spear and directed his fellows to cast spears at Odysseus. But Athena turned their spears aside. And now Odysseus directed Telemachus and Eumaeus and Philoetius to cast their spears. When they cast them with Odysseus, each one struck a man, and four of the suitors fell down. Again and again they cast their spears, and each time they slew their men. They drove those who remained from one end of the hall to the other. And the suitors fell as birds are scattered and torn by eagles.

> **slew:** (past tense of *slay*) killed

Like a lion fresh from the slaughter stood Odysseus, leaning on his spear, **glaring** round him to see if any of his foes were still alive. His eye fell on the minstrel, who was crouching in a corner near the side door. The minstrel sprang forward and threw himself at the conqueror's feet. "Spare me, Odysseus," he cried. "Telemachus knows that I sang to the suitors not of my own will. They were too many and too strong for me, and they forced me."

> **glaring:** staring fiercely

Telemachus heard him and said to his father, "The man is guiltless. Do not harm him."

"Live," said Odysseus to the minstrel, "so that you may tell others how much better good deeds are than evil."

The doors of the women's room were flung open and Eurycleia appeared. She saw Odysseus standing among the bodies of the dead, all stained with blood. She would have cried out in triumph if Odysseus had not restrained her. "Rejoice within your heart," he said, "but do not cry aloud, for it is an unholy thing to triumph over men lying dead."

And he said to the nurse, "Go now, and tell your lady that her husband has returned."

Husband and Wife Together

The old nurse Eurycleia, her feet stumbling over one another in her haste, went to the upper chamber where Penelope lay in her bed. She bent over her and called out, "Awake, dear Penelope, and see what you have longed to see for so many years. Odysseus has come back, and has slain the wicked men who have troubled you for so long."

But Penelope answered, "Surely, dear nurse, the gods have taken away your senses. Why do you mock me, waking me out of the sweetest sleep that I have had since the day when Odysseus sailed away to Troy?"

"It is true, Odysseus is here!" said the nurse. "The stranger whom we thought a beggar was Odysseus himself. Telemachus knew it all this time, but kept it from you by the command of his father."

Hearing Eurycleia say these words, Penelope sprang out of bed and put her arms round the nurse's neck. "O tell me, if he has really come home as you say, how did he, being but one, manage to slay so many?"

"I was not there," said Eurycleia. "I only heard the groaning of men as they were slain. We women sat huddled in a corner of the room with the doors closed. Then someone fetched us and I found Odysseus standing among the dead, like a lion stained with blood from the fight. And now the women are washing the hall, and he has sent me to bring you. Come with me now, lady. Now is the end of all your grief, for the husband you so longed to see has come back."

But for Penelope, joyful surprise again turned to doubt. "Dear nurse," she said, "it cannot be. Some god has taken the shape of a man to punish the suitors for the wrong they have done. Odysseus will never return home, but is lying dead in some far-off land."

"Truly, you are slow to believe," said Eurycleia. "But I can give you proof, which I saw with my own eyes—the scar of the wound that a wild boar gave him when he was but a lad. I saw it when I washed his feet, and I wanted to tell you about it, but he put his hand on my mouth and would not let me speak, for so he thought it best. On my life, it is Odysseus in the hall below."

She took Penelope by the hand and led her from the upper chamber into the hall. Odysseus was standing by a tall pillar. He waited for his wife to come and speak to him. But Penelope stood still and gazed upon him, and made no step towards him. One moment she seemed to know him, and the next moment not, for he was still in his beggar's rags.

Then Telemachus said, "Mother, is your heart so hard? Here is my father. Will you not go to him or speak with him?"

Penelope said, "My mind is amazed and I have no strength to speak, nor even to look on him face to face. If this is indeed Odysseus who has come home, a place must be prepared for him, and in time we will come to understand one another better."

Then Odysseus said to Telemachus, "Go now and wash off the stains of battle. I will stay and speak with your mother."

Then to Penelope he said, "Strange lady, is your heart indeed so hard? No other woman in the world, I think, would remain so distant from her husband who, after so much toil and so many trials, has come back after twenty years to his own home. Is there no place for me here? Must I sleep again here in the hall, on the stranger's bed?"

Penelope made no answer, for she was waiting to put this man to a final test, and Odysseus soon gave her the opportunity.

"Go, Eurycleia," Odysseus said to the old nurse, "and prepare a bed for me. I will leave this iron-hearted wife and go to my rest."

"Yes, do so, Eurycleia," said Penelope. "Take the bed he built and have it moved to another room, so that he may sleep there." She said this to test him, for the bed had a secret history known only to herself and her husband.

Then Odysseus said in anger, "Lady, what do you mean by this? How is it that my bed can be moved from place to place? There is no man living, however strong, who could move it from its place. Do you not remember how I built it? There was an olive tree growing in the inner courtyard of this house, with a trunk as wide as a pillar. Round this tree I built a room, with strong walls of stone and doors well-fitting. Then I cut off the top boughs of the olive tree and left the stump standing, which I made into a bedpost—and beginning from this I made the frame of a bed, and decorated it with gold and silver and ivory, and over the frame I stretched broad bands of leather, dyed a bright purple. Such was the bed I built, and such a bed could not be moved to this place or that."

Then Penelope knew that the man who stood before her was indeed her husband, for no one else knew how the bed had been built. She ran to him weeping and threw her arms round his neck, saying, "Do not be angry with me, Odysseus. I have long feared that someone might come here with a lying story, claiming to be my husband. But now my heart is freed from all doubts. I know that in truth you are he."

Just as the sight of land is welcome to those swimming toward the shore, when Poseidon has wrecked their ship with the fury of his winds and waves, so now was the sight of her husband welcome to Penelope as she looked upon him, and she could not tear her two fair arms from about his neck.

Then husband and wife wept together, and they told each other of things that happened in the twenty years they were apart, till dawn found them sleeping side by side.

Father and Son

The next day Odysseus said to his wife, "You and I have suffered many things for many years, and still there are many dangers to be faced. The people of Ithaca will soon hear how the suitors have been slain, and there will be great anger in their hearts, for some of them had sons and brothers among the men who are dead. I shall set everything right. But first I must go and see my father."

And so Odysseus went forth to the farm of his father, Laertes. As he drew near he saw an old man digging round a plant, whom he took to be a servant. He wore a dirty coat, patched and shabby, and a goatskin cap on his head. When Odysseus came closer, he saw that this old man was not a servant but Laertes, his own father.

And when he saw how feeble the old man was, and bent with years, Odysseus stood still, leaning against a pear tree and grieving in his heart. He hesitated, not sure whether he should go to the old man and throw his arms round him and tell him who he was, or whether he should see first if the old man would know him.

Old Laertes kept his head down as he stood digging at the plant, and he did not see Odysseus until he came near and spoke.

"Sir," said Odysseus, "you are an excellent gardener. Everything grows so well here. Fig tree, and vine, and olive, and pear—all are well cared for by your hand. But, if a stranger may say it, I see no one to care for you, to look after your old age, or to see that you are decently dressed."

As old Laertes lifted his head, Odysseus continued: "I am a stranger in Ithaca," he said. "I seek a man whom I once treated kindly—a man whose name was Odysseus. I do not know if this man is alive or dead."

Old Laertes said, "Ah, if you had been able to find him here, then you would have received true kindness in return from my son, Odysseus. But he has perished — far from his friends and his country, with neither wife nor mother nor father to weep over him."

The heart of Odysseus was moved with grief. He threw his arms around his father and kissed his head, saying, "My father, my father, look at me, for I am your long-lost son. I have come back at last after twenty years. And I have slain the suitors in my hall, paying them back in full for all the wrong that they have done."

Laertes stared at him, doubting the truth of what he heard. And old Laertes said, "If you are indeed my son, come back after all these years, show me some proof."

Then Odysseus answered, "Look now at this scar, which the wild boar made when I went hunting long ago on the mountain of Parnassus. And I will give you yet another proof, for I will tell you of the fruit trees you planted for me in this orchard when I was a little child, running along behind you — thirteen pear trees, and ten apple trees, and forty fig trees."

And Laertes knew that it was his son indeed

who stood before him—his son come back after twenty years' wandering. He cast his arms around his neck, and Odysseus caught him fainting to his breast, and led him into the house.

Within the house were Telemachus and Eumaeus the swineherd and Philoetius the cowherd. They all clasped the hand of Laertes and their words raised his spirits. And the old man went to the bath, and when he came forth, rubbed with olive oil and dressed in a fine cloak, he looked so tall and strong that his son wondered to see him. "Father," said Odysseus, "surely one of the gods has done this for you!"

Said the old hero Laertes, "Ah, my son, I wish I had my strength as **of old**, and that I had stood with you yesterday when you fought with the suitors."

> **of old:** in the past

While they were speaking, the news of how the suitors had been killed spread through the city. And those who were related to the slain men came to the courtyard of Odysseus's house and brought forth the bodies. Those who belonged to Ithaca they buried, and those who belonged to the islands they put upon ships, and sent each to his own home.

Many were angry with Odysseus for the slaying of a friend. They gathered together and cried out for vengeance. Many put on their armor and went forth to seek Odysseus. And as they went toward the city, they met with Odysseus and his following as they were coming from the house of Laertes.

Now the two groups came close to each other—on one side, the armed men, angry and seeking vengeance; and on the other, Odysseus with Telemachus, Laertes, the swineherd, and the cowherd.

Then Zeus cast down a thunderbolt from heaven, and a great figure came between them— the figure of a tall, fair, and splendid woman, whom Odysseus knew at once was the goddess Athena.

"Men of Ithaca," the goddess called out in a terrible voice, "hold your hands from fierce fighting." And the weapons fell from each man's hands.

Then the goddess came forward, taking the shape and voice of wise old Mentor, and she spoke to the people, and made them remember how Odysseus and his father before had been good kings, and how the suitors had behaved very wickedly, and had brought on their own punishment.

"And now," she said, "Odysseus is willing to forget all that is past, and to rule over you as a **just** man should. Make your peace with him."

just: fair-minded

And she herself moved their hearts to do this. So Odysseus and his people lived in peace.

So ends the story of Odysseus, who went with King Agamemnon to the wars of Troy; who made the plan of the wooden horse by which Priam's city was taken at last; who missed the way of his return, and came to the land of the lotus-eaters, and to the country of the Cyclops, and to the island of Aeolus and the house of Circe the enchantress; who heard the song of the Sirens, and sailed by terrible Scylla and Charybdis, which no other man had ever passed unharmed; who landed on the island where grazed the cattle of the Sun, and who was held for a time by the nymph Calypso—so ends the story of Odysseus, who would have been made deathless and ageless by Calypso if he had not longed always to come back to his own land and his own home and his own wife. And despite all his troubles and his toils he was fortunate, for he found a loving wife and a dutiful son and a father still alive to weep over him.

PRONUNCIATION GUIDE

In each pronunciation, the accent falls on the syllable printed in **bold** type.

Note that the letters *aa* represent the long *a* sound, as in *day* or *cake*.

A

Achilles (uh-**kil**-eez)
Aegean (ih-**gee**-uhn)
Aegyptus (ee-**jip**-tus)
Aeneas (ih-**nee**-us)
Aeneid (ih-**nee**-id)
Aeolus (**ee**-uh-lus)
Aetna (**et**-nuh)
Agamemnon (ag-uh-**mem**-nahn)
Alcinous (al-**sin**-oh-us)
Ajax Telamon (**aa**-jaks **teh**-luh-mahn)
Andromache (an-**drah**-muh-kee)
Antilochus (an-**til**-uh-kus)
Antinous (an-**tin**-oh-us)
Aphrodite (af-ruh-**die**-tee)
Apollo (uh-**pah**-low)
Ares (**air**-eez)
Arete (ahr-**ee**-tee)
Argos (**ahr**-gos)
Athena (uh-**thee**-nuh)
Aulis (**aw**-lus)

Pronunciation Guide

B

Balius (**bal**-ee-us)
Briseis (bry-**see**-iss)

C

Calchas (**kal**-kus)
Calypso (kuh-**lip**-so)
Cassandra (kuh-**san**-druh)
Charybdis (kuh-**rib**-dis)
Chryseis (kry-**see**-iss)
Chryses (**kry**-seez)
Circe (**sur**-see)
Crete (kreet)
Cyclops (**sye**-klops)

D

Delphi (**del**-fye)
Demodocus (dih-**mah**-duh-kus)
Diomedes (die-uh-**mee**-deez)

E

Eris (**air**-iss)
Eumaeus (yoo-**mee**-us)
Euryalus (yuh-**rye**-uh-lus)
Eurycleia (yoor-ih-**klee**-uh)
Eurymachus (yuh-**rim**-uh-kus)

H

Hades (**hay**-deez)
Halitherses (hal-lih-**thur**-seez)
Hector (**hek**-ter)
Hecuba (**heh**-kyuh-buh)
Helen (**hel**-uhn)
Hephaestus (hih-**feh**-stus)
Hera (**hair**-uh)
Hermes (**her**-meez)

I

Iliad (**il**-lee-uhd)
Ilium (**il**-lee-um)
Ino (**eye**-noh)
Iris (**eye**-ris)
Ithaca (**ih**-thih-kuh)

L

Laertes (lay-**uhr**-teez or lay-**air**-teez)
Laodamas (lay-**ahd**-uh-mus)

M

Melanthius (meh-**lan**-thee-us)
Menelaus (meh-nuh-**lay**-us)
Mycenae (my-**see**-nee)
Myrmidons (**muhr**-mih-dahnz)

PRONUNCIATION GUIDE

N

Nausicaa (**nah**-sih-kuh or nah-sih-**kay**-uh)
Nestor (**nes**-ter)
Noemon (**no**-eh-mahn)

O

Odysseus (oh-**dis**-ee-us)
Odyssey (**ah**-duh-see)
Oenone (ee-**no**-nee)

P

Palamedes (pal-uh-**mee**-deez)
Pandarus (**pan**-duh-rus)
Paris (**pair**-iss)
Patroclus (puh-**troh**-klus)
Peisistratus (pie-**sis**-truh-tus)
Peleus (**pee**-lee-us or **peel**-yoos)
Penelope (puh-**nel**-uh-pee)
Penthesilea (pen-thuh-sih-**lee**-uh)
Phaeacia (fee-**aa**-shuh)
Philoetius (fih-**lee**-shyus)
Phoenix (**fee**-nicks)
Polyphemus (pah-luh-**fee**-mus)
Poseidon (puh-**sye**-dun)
Priam (**pry**-uhm)
Pyrrhus (**peer**-us)

S

Scylla (**sil**-luh)
Sinon (**sye**-nahn)
Skyros (**sky**-rus)

T

Telemachus (tuh-**leh**-muh-kus)
Thetis (**thee**-tis)
Thessaly (**theh**-suh-lee)

X

Xanthus (**zan**-thuhs)

Z

Zeus (zoos)

Cover and Title Page Illustration by
Ivan Pesic

Text Illustrations by
De Luan / Alamy Stock Photo / 100
FALKENSTEINFOTO / Alamy Stock Photo / 55, 192
Heritage Image Partnership Ltd / Alamy Stock Photo / 162
Historic Collection / Alamy Stock Photo / 88
History and Art Collection / Alamy Stock Photo / 94
INTERFOTO / Alamy Stock Photo / 44, 57, 108, 120
Ivan Pesic / iii, 267
Ivy Close Images / Alamy Stock Photo / 28, 112, 131, 167, 203, 216, 240, 251
Nikolay Staykov / Alamy Stock Photo / 2
Quagga Media / Alamy Stock Photo / 70
The Picture Art Collection / Alamy Stock Photo / 6, 35, 146, 182
World History Archive / Alamy Stock Photo / 38

TEXT SOURCES

This adaptation builds on the work of many authors from a century or more ago, especially Alfred J. Church (for the *Iliad*) and Padraic Colum (for the *Odyssey*).

Baldwin, James. "The Golden Apple," in *A Story of the Golden Age*. New York: Charles Scribner's Sons, 1905.

---"The Fall of Troy," in *Thirty More Famous Stories Retold*. New York: American Book Co., 1905.

Butler, Samuel, translator. *The Odyssey*. London: A. C. Fifield, 1900.

Church, Alfred J. *The Iliad for Boys and Girls*. New York: Macmillan, 1907.

---*The Odyssey for Boys and Girls*. New York: Macmillan, 1906.

---*Stories from Homer*. London: Seeley and Co., 1907.

Clarke, Michael. *The Story of Troy*. New York: American Book Company, 1897.

Colum, Padraic. *The Adventures of Odysseus and the Tale of Troy*. New York: Macmillan, 1918.

Dyer, Franklin B. and Mary J. Brady, editors. "Homer," in *The Merrill Readers: Sixth Reader*. New York: Charles E. Merrill Co., 1916.

Havell, H. L. *Stories from the Odyssey*. London: George G. Harrap and Co., 1908.

Peabody, Josephine Preston. *Old Greek Folk Stories Told Anew*. Boston: Houghton, Mifflin and Co., 1897.

Tappan, Eva March, editor. *The Children's Hour, Vol. III: Stories from the Classics*. Boston: Houghton Mifflin and Co., 1907.